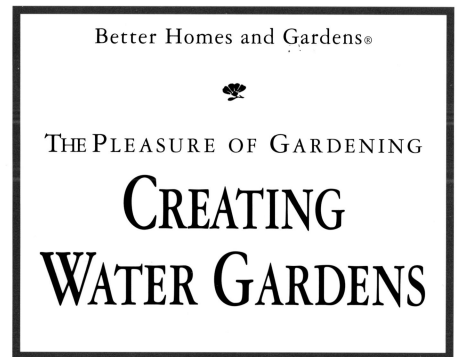

Better Homes and Gardens®

THE PLEASURE OF GARDENING

CREATING WATER GARDENS

Better Homes and Gardens®

THE PLEASURE OF GARDENING

CREATING WATER GARDENS

BY MARY MOODY

Better Homes and Gardens® Books
Des Moines

CONTENTS

Introduction

Every aspect of creating a garden is fascinating, from the enriching of the soil to the selection of suitable plants. Garden lovers, the world over, take great pleasure in all the possibilities and challenges of making a beautiful garden. There is no doubt that some people become hooked on one particular theme or approach, and those who have experimented with creating water gardens often fall into this category. Whatever the theme or style, there is great satisfaction in successfully landscaping a pond, a stream or a waterfall, and in cultivating all those delightful species that thrive in the water or its immediate surroundings. In my own garden, the pond has a purely practical application: it is the home of a small flock of ducks who keep my vegetable and flower gardens free from slugs and snails. The ducks are inclined to trample the pond edges and stir up the water, but their contribution to the ecological balance of the gardens makes them worth the mess!

In more sophisticated gardens I have always admired the clever, and often artistic, use of water as a landscaping device. In terms of creativity, bringing water into a garden inevitably gives gardeners one of their best opportunities for self-expression. Whether modern or traditional in design, simple or complex in execution, fountains and waterfalls can often be considered works of art in the way they combine the elements of moving water and light.

Yet perhaps the most interesting water gardens are those which emulate nature, and capture the atmosphere of a wild stream or brook. Here the skillful use of rock is vital if the garden is to appear truly natural. The Japanese have mastered the art of arranging rocks so that they nestle into the ground as though they have been in place for hundreds of years. A tremendous amount of time and patience is required to develop this skill, but the completed garden will no doubt bring rewards for many years to come.

This title in *The Pleasure of Gardening* series looks at all aspects of creating a successful water garden, from the modest to the magnificent. It will inspire the enthusiast with ideas and practical information on how to construct a simple garden pond and how to maintain a healthy water environment.

LEFT: A traditional English walled garden, where a central pond is the main feature.

THE WATER
GARDEN IN
HISTORY

Traditional Uses of Water in Garden Design

If we cherish the belief that a garden must be a place of restfulness as well as a place of visual beauty, then water must surely be the essential ingredient. Of all nature's elements, water is the one that brings a feeling of peace to the landscape. It plays on all the senses—sight, sound, smell, touch, and taste—and offers a cornucopia of design possibilities in gardens of all sizes and styles. On a grand scale, imagine a country garden complete with a lake edged by gently sloping banks, a meandering stream spanned by a Monet-style bridge; on a minimal scale, think of a Japanese stone water bowl providing a cool resting place for native birds.

PREVIOUS PAGE: The formal water terrace at Blenheim Palace in Oxfordshire, England, is surrounded by neatly clipped box hedges and topiary. This garden was first established in 1705, although it has been redesigned several times. Water is one of the most dramatic features.

OPPOSITE: The classic formal beauty of La Fondation Ephrussi de Rothschild, in the south of France, combines a variety of elements including stepped cascades and a rectangular pool with a central single-jet fountain. The water garden is designed to be viewed from one end, looking up to the domed pavilion.

The role of water in garden design has a long and illustrious history, both in the East and in Western gardens. During the time of Plato, public fountains adorned parks and temple groves, while sacred fountains and shrines to Pan, nymphs, and the muses nestled in private garden sanctuaries. Homer's *Odyssey* describes the Sanctuary of Nymphs at Ithaca, where streams tumbled over rocks and boulders to a shrine known as a Nymphaeum, dedicated to the nymphs and complete with fountains designed to represent a natural grotto. Ultimately, the development of hydraulic engineering and aqueducts in Rome produced many ornamental fountains and water gardens including Hadrian's villa at Tivoli, which boasted an extravagant display of waterworks in the form of streams, canals, fountains, and pools. Even today in the Vatican you can see the wondrous gilt Byzantine fountain La Pigna, in the shape of a pine cone sprinkling water. In the Paradise Gardens of Islam water was an integral feature, with water canals, representing the 'four rivers of paradise', dividing garden plots.

The luxurious villa gardens of rural Pompeii are recorded in wall paintings and engravings that show elaborate trellises and urns. Rills (small constructed rivulets) are mentioned in literature describing the period, as are columned terraces with fountains and deep channels that formed artificial rivers. The beauty of these gardens, buried beneath volcanic ash and pumice for 16 centuries, was uncovered in the early 18th century, when workmen digging a well accidentally stumbled upon the remains. The region was rich in natural beauty; and water must have been plentiful to have supported such a variety of ornamental water gardens.

Water was also a powerful theme in the gardens of the Mogul Empire, usually around mosques and places where people bathed. In China and Japan the influence of water was pervasive; no Chinese garden was designed without a combination of water and mountains. The landscapes of these two countries are noted for their use of water: streams, springs, ponds, and lakes cleverly designed to emulate wild nature. The use of boulders and rocks, and the selection of carefully scaled plant material, add to the beauty and serenity of these gardens.

In Egypt the gardens of the Pharaohs and other members of the wealthy elite had two priorities—water and shade—to combat the relentless heat. Gardens were an oasis of beauty, with scented shrubs

ABOVE: Often the most effective designs are the most simple, like this trough and fountain at Hestercombe Gardens in Somerset, England. The walled garden features symmetrical areas of lawn, with water troughs that are planted with a variety of moisture-loving plants including iris and the water forget-me-not (Myosotis scorpioides).

forming an understory to shade trees. Walled gardens, established to create a cooler microclimate, contained simple rectangular pools, with spouts from the roof playing water into the pool, where ornamental fish were probably kept. An Egyptian garden plan discovered in the tomb of a high official at Thebes demonstrates a quite sophisticated irrigation system, as well as vine-covered places and terraces of sycamore and palm trees.

In European gardens of the Middle Ages a fountain or water basin was considered essential, and was usually located in the middle of a walled area. Monastery gardens, where herbs were grown for medicinal purposes, are well recorded; and here water was also important as a religious symbol of purification. Gardens were practical as well as spiritual features, producing vegetables and fruits for the families who dwelt inside the walls and cloisters.

A more classical or formal approach to water garden design can be seen in the Italian gardens of the Renaissance, including the magnificent Villa d'Este at Tivoli which included such sumptuous sights as the 'Pathway of a Hundred Fountains', considered by many to be the most imaginative use of water in landscape history. The parterre gardens of Tuscany, both modest and grand, have inspired many contemporary landscapers, and here water gardens are a recurring theme. Symmetrical pools and sculptural fountains add to the more formal approach. Beds edged with clipped trees and potted lemon trees are common accoutrements.

Many garden enthusiasts know and appreciate the work of the famous Le

ABOVE: A small, circular formal pool used as the focal point of a well planned and planted garden. Between the beds a smooth grass pathway leads the eye from a vine-covered pergola to the pool planted with waterlilies (Nymphaea *sp.) and bogbean* (Menyanthes trifoliata).

Notre family of French gardeners, whose designs were employed over several generations during the 16th and 17th centuries. They used water extensively throughout their gardens, but were frequently frustrated by the lack of sufficient water pressure for highly elaborate fountain displays. They made effective use of canals rather than waterfalls or cascades, and their great work includes the magnificent gardens of Versailles. Water for the complex fountain system at Versailles was stored in huge holding tanks; the force of gravity brought the fountains alive. Despite the size of the tanks the water was quickly exhausted each time it was released, requiring regular refilling.

Another outstanding example of French garden design is the Chateau Vaux-le-Vicompte, in which water has been used on a grand, if somewhat theatrical, scale. Fountains and canals are a strong feature, however it is the larger than life Grand Cascade which strikes one as the most spectacular attraction.

Also in France, Claude Monet, a leader of the Impressionist school of painters, kept a beautiful garden at Giverny filled with rambling roses, poppies, blue corn cockle and bright yellow daisies. This garden, in particular the water garden, provided the inspiration for much of his later work, including the famous waterlily series of paint-

OPPOSITE: A Monet-style painted timber bridge spans a peaceful lake, surrounded by deciduous trees and edged by hydrangeas and a variety of rushes and sedges. A lake of this size can sustain a jetty and a boat for added enjoyment of the water.

ings. The house and gardens have been restored and are open to the public.

Dutch gardens were tremendously influential in the evolution of landscape architecture in Northern Europe in the 16th, 17th, and 18th centuries. Again water was a vital element, from the classical canal gardens with their rectilinear layout framed by canals and trees to the Dutch Regency gardens such as Waterland, near Haarlem, which features a labyrinthine design of avenues and a lake large enough for sailing boats.

In England the most notable use of water is to be found in public parks and gardens, such as Birkenhead Park, in Liverpool, which was transformed from an unattractive swampy tract of land into a series of formal and informal gardens set around two large lakes, each containing an island. At the time, 1843, the excavation of the lakes was a considerable engineering feat. Another fantastic example is at Chatsworth, Derbyshire—surely one of the grandest houses in England—where the gardens display water in an infinite variety of applications, from lakes and fountains to waterfalls, generally on a very large scale.

In these large-scale water gardens grand pavilions were sometimes built, such as the one at Stourhead, with its dome and majestic stone columns. These grand structures could be considered a little over-theatrical, designed as scaled-down versions of classic Greek and Roman temples. However, they afforded fantastic views of the lakes beside which they were placed, and provided the wealthy with a venue in which to sip wine and enjoy the garden. The pavilions were also used for fishing and boating

expeditions, and as changing rooms for swimmers.

The use of water in modern landscape design has been simplified by the development of synthetic means of waterproofing and advanced techniques with pumps and plumbing. Using the available technology it is possible to incorporate water effectively in a tremendous variety of ways; from simple natural rock pools to dramatic cascades and fountains. The joy now is in the knowledge that there are so many possibilities; even in a small city courtyard or a suburban garden, one can have the pleasure of water nearby. I personally prefer the notion of a multi-functional water garden—perhaps a lilypond that is large enough to support a couple of ducks, which can effectively remove snails from the kitchen garden. Or a large natural rock pool that is filtered for swimming and landscaped to appear part of the surrounding environment.

Be it strictly ornamental or practical in application, water in the garden will provide great enjoyment and beauty, regardless of climate or garden style. But even in regions where it is in plentiful supply water should be used conservatively, especially if it is for pure ornamentation. All modern water gardens can be designed to recirculate water, so that the one volume is used over and over again.

This book aims to inspire you with imaginative ideas on how to use water in the garden; as well as providing practical information on basic construction methods, water ecology, and suitable plants for deep water, marginal areas, and poolside landscaping.

STYLE
OPTIONS

A Central Fountain

A fountain is a simple way of introducing moving water to a garden, without the need for elaborate recirculating streams or waterfalls. A fountain forces water through a small aperture so that it creates a jet or spray in the air. As in all water features, the play of water and light is an important element. Fountains should be located where they can be appreciated from all sides, and where the sunlight will catch the moving water to produce a shimmering effect that excites the senses.

Looking back into horticultural history we find fountains documented as a feature in gardens from the time of the Emperor Hadrian, whose famous villa

PREVIOUS PAGE: The charming water garden at Tintinhull House in Somerset, England. This garden has several distinct areas, including an azalea garden and a fountain garden, linked to a series of courtyard gardens. It is essentially formal in layout, yet manages to achieve a relaxed atmosphere through informal planting in a free-flowing design.

OPPOSITE: In formal design, symmetry is often a strong element, as in this simple circular pond that is centrally located in a pleasant walled garden. Fruiting trees have been used ornamentally through the edging beds, and a lush circular lawn emphasizes the shape of the pond. In this garden, potted plants include fuchsias, geraniums, and balsam.

outside Rome had a variety of them. Another famous example, dating back to the 11th century, is the Court of the Lions in the Allambra at Granada, in southern Spain. Here 12 beautifully carved lions form an amazing fountain, with slender jets of water emerging from their mouths.

The style of a fountain can vary tremendously, from a simple spurt or jet of water emerging from the middle of a pond to a sophisticated sculpture that is the focal point of a formal courtyard garden. There are wall-mounted fountains in the classical Italian style; birdbaths with shimmering spouts; foaming water spouts; traditional tiered fountains whose water flows into a series of larger and smaller water bowls; glazed ceramic or bronze fountains that are artworks in their own right; and delicate fan sprays that rely on every exhilarating water droplet catching the sunlight. The pace of water movement can also vary, from a high spurt to a slow stream; or be automatically programmed to change from fast to slow in order to create a random 'dancing water' effect.

Unlike the water gardens of the Villa D'Este, in Italy, where a river was harnessed to provide the water power for the myriad gushing displays, modern fountains need not be extravagant in water consumption. Using a simple submersible pump the same water can be circulated effectively, and will not be wasted unless high wind sends the water spray flying in all directions. For this reason the fountain should be positioned in a sheltered place, away from strong prevailing winds, and have a catchment pond at the base whose diameter is at least twice the height of the water jet. (That is, a spray that is 3 feet high will need to be surrounded below by a pond that is at least 6 feet across.) If the fountain is in a windy place the catchment pond should be even larger, or the surrounding area will become wet and slippery and a great deal of the water will be lost. A grate around the circumference of the pond can be used to return water to the recirculation system. In some cases lawn can be planted that will benefit from the occasional extra spray of water. In more sophisticated water gardens the fountain spray can be regulated according to the wind velocity, reducing the height of the spray on particularly windy days!

Fountains can also be lit for evening enjoyment. If the lighting is high voltage an electrician will be needed for the installation; however, quite effective low voltage lighting can be installed by the average handyperson. The effect of light on water at night can be quite dramatic—whether the lights are positioned underwater or overhead—creating mood and atmosphere in the garden.

A Central Fountain

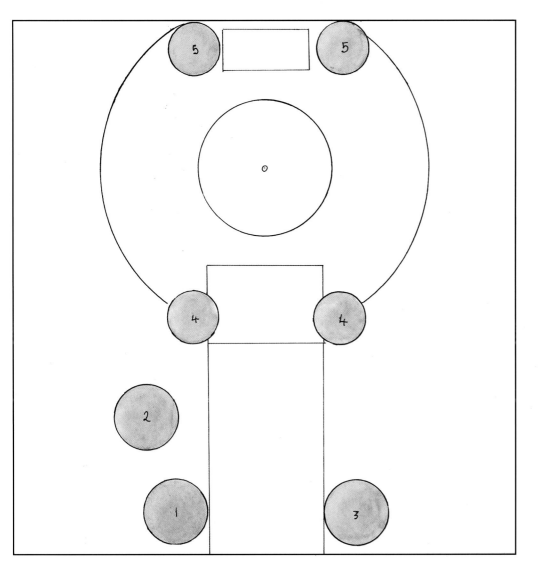

Key to Planting Plan

1. Fuchsia 'Jack Shahan' H. 18 inches
2. Fuchsia 'Cascade' H. 18 inches
3. Fuchsia 'Rough Silk' H. 2 feet
4. Impatiens (Balsam) H. 2 feet
5. *Pelargonium 'caligula'* (Geranium)
H. 8 inches

H. = Height

A shady and cool retreat, where water is a major feature. This small, formal central fountain is easy to achieve because the elements are so simple: a shallow, circular pool edged with bricks, and a single jet of water powered by a small submersible pump. Grass surrounds the pool, repeating its circular shape, then raised beds of trees, shrubs, and perennials add texture and shade. Potted fuchsias, geraniums and balsam bloom over many weeks in summer and early autumn.

A Lily Pond

A shimmering pond of waterlilies (nymphaea) in flower is a beautiful sight to behold: large floating leaves cradling droplets of water and bold, cup-shaped fragrant flowers in a wide range of exquisite hues. The lily pond has long been a popular choice in both formal and informal gardens, providing a perfect use for still water. Indeed, these robust plants will always do best in a still pond or water garden, as long as there is plenty of warm sunshine to boost their growth and flower production.

The genus nymphaea contains both deciduous and evergreen perennials and can be divided into two main groups: those that are hardy and suited to growing in most climates and conditions; and those that are tender and originate in the tropics and are suited only to cultivation in warmer climates. Both groups include many varieties, ranging from small growers that are ideal for the most

OPPOSITE: Waterlilies can be grown in any pond that gets sufficient direct sunlight for them to flower. There are small-growing as well as vigorous-growing species; the variety selected should match the size of the pond or lake. The broad lilypads help to keep the water cool by providing shade, which reduces algae growth.

compact courtyard water garden to more vigorous plants which can quickly cover an area of several square yards. The waterlily 'Aurora' is a delightful deciduous plant that is hardy and has star-shaped, semi-double flowers that are 2 inches across, emerging as pale cream buds deepening to yellow, then orange, and finally a rich shade of red. With a spread of only 30 inches, it is an ideal waterlily for a small water garden. On the other hand, the vigorous deciduous N. alba spreads to 10 feet on the water's surface, with deep green glossy leaves and pure white sweetly scented flowers that can measure 4 inches across. As a massed planting in a large pond or pool it creates a spectacular effect, especially if plantings of moisture-loving plants at the water's edge echo the green and white theme! These varieties are typical of those admired by gardeners who like the semi-double flowers and comparative ease of cultivation.

The large leaves of the waterlily, which float on the surface, are practical as well as beautiful because they provide a shady water environment that prevents the excessive growth of algae and provides a pleasant habitat for fish. Most varieties are fairly easy to cultivate, providing care is taken at the time of

establishing the plants in the pond. A common mistake is to plunge potted plants directly into the water, which can be fatal if the temperature is very cold. They need to be introduced gradually by filling the pond slowly around them, in the beginning barely covering the container and then adding water over a period of weeks until the pond is filled.

Waterlilies can be planted directly into rich soil at the base of the pond, providing it is not too deep (3 feet maximum for the larger varieties), or planted in pots that are submerged. In deeper ponds the pots can be elevated by standing them on another inverted pot. The soil surface can be protected from disturbance by fish by covering it with a layer of fine rocks or gravel. While waterlilies can be grown successfully in pools or ponds with recirculating fountains or waterfalls, they resent fast-flowing water and are not suited to streams.

In most climates the pond is best located in the sunniest and most open part of the garden, away from overhanging trees that will litter the water with leaf fall. The only exception to this occurs in regions that experience very hot summers, when the midday sun may be a little harsh. Some nearby tree or shrub cover will solve this problem.

ABOVE: It is little wonder that waterlilies (Nymphaea sp.) are the most popular and widely grown plants for the water garden. The exquisite summer flowers are perfectly offset by the spreading lilypads, which shimmer with delicate droplets of water.

RIGHT: Enclosed by clipped hedges and beds of flowering roses, the formal pool at Tintinhull House in Somerset, England, is popular with garden lovers who visit when the gardens are open in spring and summer.

A Lily Pond

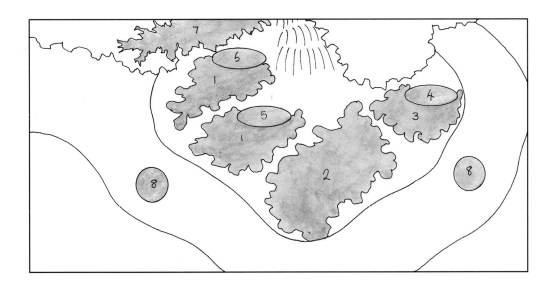

Key to Planting Plan

1. Nymphaea 'Gonnere' S. 5 feet
2. Nymphaea 'Attraction' S. 6 ½ feet
3. Nymphaea 'Blue Beauty' S. 8 feet
4. *Iris ensata* H. 2 feet
5. *Ranunculus lingua* (Buttercup) H. 3 feet
6. *Acorus calamus* H. 1 foot

H. = Height
S. = Spread

A warm, sunny location will be needed if waterlilies (*Nymphaea* sp.) are to be grown successfully. There are many different varieties to suit all sizes of water garden, from dwarf species for small pools, to the more vigorous growers that will fill a large pond or lake. Here several varieties have been combined with taller water plants such as *Acorus calamus, Ranunculus lingua* and *Iris ensata.* Avoid planting deciduous trees or shrubs overhanging a lily pond, because their falling leaves will cause problems in the water when they decompose.

A Waterfall

Of all the ways that water can be used in the landscape, the waterfall is the most dramatic and appealing. Here we see the movement of water at its best, from a delicate trickle to a rushing torrent; all the sights and sounds of rippling water in focus. Indeed, the sounds of a waterfall are so soothing and diverting that they can be used as a landscaping device to combat surrounding noise pollution, creating a sense of peace in an environment that might otherwise be noisy and unpleasant.

Waterfalls and cascades were used by the Romans to cool the air and excite the senses. Formal Italian gardens in the 16th century also featured extravagant cascades or 'water staircases', some of which can still be seen today. Indeed, through history the use of moving water in the garden was generally associated with wealth, as such gardens often required the diversion of a natural waterway to achieve the desired effect.

When planning a waterfall first consider the size of the garden, as the scale of this feature must be in proportion to its surroundings. Another factor is the volume of water to be moved, which can vary considerably. In certain Japanese-style water gardens the water flow is no more than a moist shimmer, which can be designed to occur naturally without the assistance of pumps or a recirculation system. In more adventurous garden design a large volume of water may need to be carried from a catchment pond back up to a header pool, and this will require a strong pump and substantial power usage. The volume of water will be determined by the width and height of the waterfall and also the size of the header and catchment pools.

The most pleasing waterfalls make good use of stone and rock to flank the falls and to provide a 'mirror' to the water. There are various ways in which rocks can be used. A large vertical rock may be used as a fallstone, over which the water flows; a smaller rounded rock may be used as a splash stone at the base of the falls to create interesting water patterns and to divide the water into two channels in the catchment pond. There are no hard-and-fast rules about the placement of rocks; however, from a purely aesthetic point of view, certain tricks are useful to create the right natural balance. In essence, the framing rocks on either side of the water flow should be visually more prominent than the waterfall itself. Large stones at the top of the waterfall, and at its base, will be needed to create a balance. The fall should nestle within the stone framework, rather than trying to dominate it. Even taking into account the design limitations there is great scope for creativity in the use of rocks and water, and also in the use of plants to frame and soften the finished effect.

Apart from the benefits of the sight and sound of moving water, a waterfall can create a healthier environment within a garden pond. It helps to keep oxygen moving through the water which in turn makes it a better place for fish and water plants. Very fast flowing water will not, however, suit certain plants—it may dislodge their roots or wash them to one end of the pond.

In water gardens in which the water is not recirculated 24 hours a day but only switched on for effect, the catchment pond must be large enough to hold the entire water volume when the falls are still. An overflow pipe may be required to carry excess water to other parts of the garden so that it is not wasted.

OPPOSITE: The magical quality of moving water is never more dramatically displayed than in a natural waterfall. In this garden the water flow is quite rapid, creating a moist air environment for the cultivation of ferns and other foliage plants that thrive in this setting. Large rocks and boulders have been used effectively, forming the sides and base of the waterfall.

A Waterfall

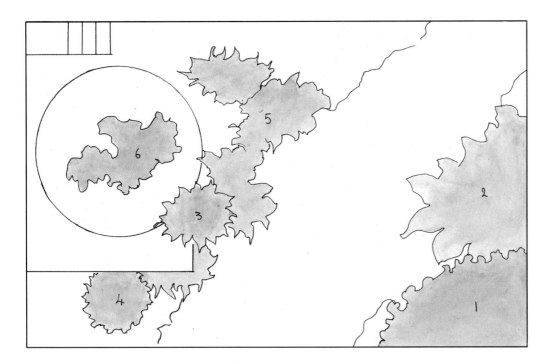

Key to Planting Plan

1. Tropaeolum (Nasturtiums) H. 8 inches
2. *Monstera deliciosa* (Fruit salad plant)
H. 20 feet
3. *Zantedeschia* sp. (Arum lily) H. 3 feet
4. Impatiens (Balsam) H. 2 feet
5. Ferns (mixed according to the climate)
6. *Nymphaea* sp. (Waterlilies) S. 6 ¹/₂ feet

H. = Height
S. = Spread

The most dramatic of all water garden effects are waterfalls or rapids, where the sights and sounds of fast flowing water bring great drama to the garden. This style of water garden takes a lot of planning and designing, and will require one or two aquatic pumps to keep the water moving steadily from the lower pond back up to the head of the falls. Surrounding plants will benefit from the moist conditions created as the water splashes and sprays over the rock cascades. Select plants that like these humid conditions, such as ferns which thrive where both the soil and air are moisture-laden.

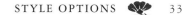

A Courtyard Water Garden

Courtyards are wonderful settings in which to garden. They provide a warm and sheltered micro-climate in which a tremendous range of plants can be cultivated with ease. The walls of the courtyard can be used for growing climbing species, with perhaps one wall used as a special feature for a fountain or small water garden. Being so sheltered, fountains are ideal in this situation, and sprays of water will not be wasted as they often are in more exposed locations.

Noise pollution can be overcome within the confines of a courtyard, especially if the walls are of brick or stone. Inside, the sound of moving water from a fountain or small water-fall will enhance the feeling of peace and separation from the hustle and bustle of the outside world. The calming sounds of the flowing water, in fact, will be magnified as they bounce off the interior walls, adding to the feeling of privacy.

Throughout history water has been used as an integral part of courtyard gardens. In hot climates, especially, it helped to keep out the pervasive heat and dust, to keep courtyards cool and pleasant retreats. In Islamic courtyards stone, marble, or mosaic was often a construction feature, softened by trees and shrubs and by water in the form of peaceful pools or simple fountains. These water gardens were generally placed in the middle of the courtyard, to provide a focus of attention when viewed from the surrounding arcades.

If you are planning a courtyard water garden consider the dimensions of the area, because the pool, pond, or fountain should be in scale with the size of the courtyard. While the water will probably be the main focal point of the garden, it should remain in harmony with the garden. Also consider the points from which the water will be viewed. Often courtyards are overlooked from the house, and therefore the pond should be located so that it can be seen and enjoyed from that vantage point.

In a formal courtyard, take advantage of the wall space to incorporate a small

OPPOSITE: Courtyards provide warm sheltered conditions that make it possible to grow a wide range of plants that require some protection from the cold or from strong winds. Water helps create a warm moist microclimate, here demonstrated in a simple, brick-paved circular pond that features a central water spout. Ferns and ground covers thrive, while built-up beds of shrubs and perennials enjoy the sheltered environment.

fountain, such as those classical cement or terracotta lion's heads through which a gently curved arch of water flows. Use a trellis against the wall for some climbing roses that will frame the fountain—as well as filling the garden with fragrance.

A garden bench, located near the pool, will provide a place from which the sights and sounds of moving water can be enjoyed. If the ecology of the pool is in balance it will not be a breeding ground for mosquitoes, which can sometimes make sitting near a water

garden quite an ordeal. If the water garden is informal in design, soften the edges with plants that thrive in the sheltered conditions of the courtyard—ferns and primulas are particularly attractive, providing the soil conditions are rich and moist.

ABOVE: The walls of the courtyard can be used for growing many climbing plants, such as these charming yellow roses.

OPPOSITE: Smooth sandstone paving stones add to the elegance of this courtyard garden, complete with a formal rectangular pool that has been planted with waterlilies and azolla.

A Courtyard Water Garden

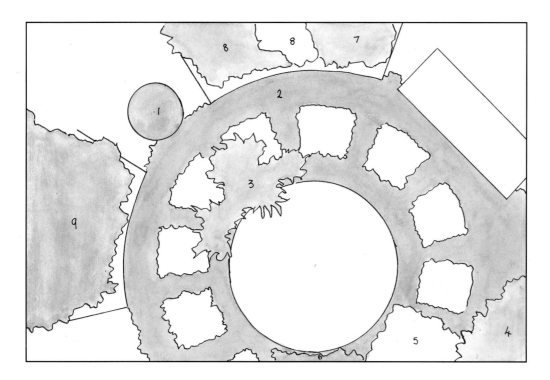

Key to Planting Plan

1. *Zantedeschia* sp. (Arum lily) H. 2 feet
2. *Thymus* sp. (Thyme) H. & S. 8 inches
3. Mixed ferns
4. *Primula* sp. H. 5 inches–8 inches
5. *Anemone blands* (Windflower)
H. 3 1/4 feet
6. *Viola* sp. (Pansies) H. 4 inches
7. *Acer palmatum* (Weeping maple)
8. *Azalea racemosum* H. 8 feet
9. *Azalea mollis* H. 6 1/2 feet

H. = Height
S. = Spread

Courtyard gardens are sheltered from strong winds, with walls that trap the sun to create a warm microclimate for growing a wide variety of plants. In this protected garden, a brick-edged circular pond is surrounded by lush growth. Flat paving stones are interplanted with ground hugging thyme (*Thymus* sp.) and clumps of ferns, which enjoy the warm, moist environment. A handsome urn of arum lilies (*Zantedeschia* sp.) and a carved stone bench are pleasant accessories, while built-up brick beds of azaleas, weeping maples (*Acer palmatum*) and primulas enjoy the good drainage that these conditions provide.

A Contemporary Water Garden

Water gardens can be as adventurous and modern as the latest architecture, allowing the imagination to explore all the ways in which the properties of water can be combined with surrounding textures, shapes, and forms. In many modern settings construction of the water garden is planned to coincide with that of the house, and is an integral part of the overall design theme. Contemporary architectural design often incorporates water as a feature—indoors as well as in the garden. Water can be used to link the interior of the house to the garden or to an enclosed courtyard or swimming pool area.

Water gardens may differ from 'nature' but they still satisfy our senses. Modern designs for waterfalls,

OPPOSITE: A stylized pebble water garden that is formal in design, centrally positioned in a peaceful walled garden. Neatly clipped shrubs have been arranged symmetrically to emphasize the formal setting. A vine-covered pergola will eventually provide shade so that the garden can be enjoyed in comfort.

fountains, streams, or pools will still contain all the soothing qualities that the introduction of water brings in more traditional or 'natural' settings. Indeed, contemporary design ideas, combined with water, can produce powerful and dramatic effects, especially if sculpture and modern spot or low-voltage lighting are involved.

In well-designed buildings the use of water and glass can be as cooling as air-conditioning. A fine trickle of water down the outside of a plate glass window overlooking the garden will help to reduce the internal temperature of the house, as well as having a psychological cooling effect. Water gardens can be built indoors, as a sculptural feature or surrounded by a variety of potted ferns and foliage plants to continue the restful theme.

Sculptural water gardens can be as free in form as you wish, without any rules or restrictions in design. In many ways it is easier to build a high-tech contemporary water garden than to try cleverly to imitate nature to perfection. The choice of construction materials is as wide as the imagination—from stone

and cement to glass, plastics, timber, and metals such as stainless steel or bronze. Water can be still, but it is more fascinating if allowed to spill, cascade, or spray in wall fountains, spill fountains, or geometric tiered fountains. Or if used in splash sculpture, where a major work of art has water flowing in, through, or around it.

Fish can easily be incorporated into a contemporary garden, providing a healthy water environment is created for them. If the fish are to be viewed through glass, filters will be needed to maintain water clarity. A modern biological filter can be used to keep the water crystal clear, and will allow a greater number of fish to be supported in a given volume of water.

A formal approach has been taken in this contemporary water garden. A rectangular shallow pond set into a paved courtyard has been filled with smooth river stones, and then landscaped with clipped box shrubs in wooden tubs. While very modern in design, it also has classic elements of the wonderful Italian water gardens found in Tuscany.

A Contemporary Water Garden

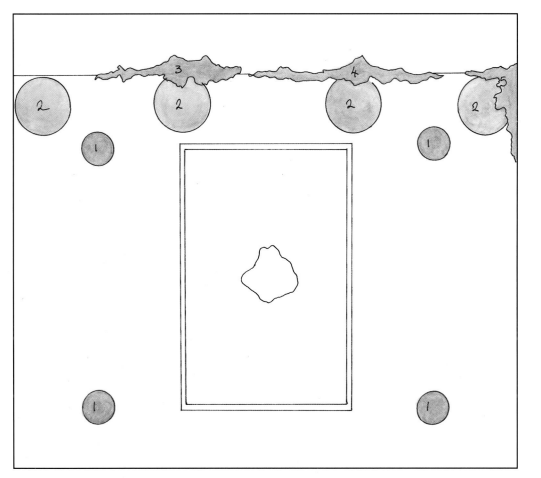

Key to Planting Scheme

1. *Buxus sempervirens* (Box)
H. 16 feet unclipped
2. Hebe H. 1 foot
3. *Solanum jasminoides* 'Album'
4. *Wisteria floribunda*
5. Clematis 'Nelly Moser'

H. = Height

A charming contemporary courtyard, where a central pond of smooth river stones is the main feature. The beauty of this garden is its absolute minimum of maintenance, with paving covering most surfaces, except several places where plants have been strategically positioned. A pergola covered with clematis, wisteria and *Solanum jasminoides* will shade the seating area in summer, while allowing the warmth of the sun's rays through in winter. Four formal tubs of neatly clipped box shrubs (*Buxus sempervirens*) frame the rectangular pool, and circular beds planted with white flowering hebe are a most effective finishing touch.

A Woodland Stream

It is possible to establish a woodland garden in a variety of settings—not only in a rambling country estate. The feeling of woodland can easily be recreated in a much more limited landscape with the imaginative use of established trees and ground-level plantings. A classic example occurs when bulbs are grown at the base of large deciduous trees, forming a striking carpet in early spring. This simple planting method helps to recreate the untamed nature of the woodland.

A similar approach can be taken in the construction of a stream in a woodland garden. The surrounding trees will be the main design feature, positioned to follow the stream but hopefully not to drop too

OPPOSITE: Streams can take many forms, from natural watercourses that meander through a woodland garden to more contrived designs. Pebbles and smooth river stones have been effectively used in this small stream, so that the water slowly trickles into a rock-lined pool. Nearby beds have been extensively planted with perennials and shrubs that thrive in the rich moist growing conditions.

many leaves into its waters. In nature a stream takes a meandering path; so too should your replica. An artificial stream will need to be lined to prevent bank erosion and water seepage. All the construction materials mentioned in Chapter Three can be used to establish a small natural stream using a pump to circulate the water. When not in use, the water for the stream can be stored in an underground tank or sump, so that there is little or no wastage.

Rocks and stones can be a practical and beautiful addition to stream building: to strenghten the banks or, in a shallow stream, to help create a babbling effect as the water passes over them. In a fast-flowing stream rapids can be developed by placing large stones or boulders that dam up the water, causing it to bounce and foam over the obstacles. This effect can be created in quite shallow streams and will add drama to the garden.

People fortunate enough to have a natural stream or brook running through their property will enjoy the pleasure of selecting plants that bring variety to the setting. Avoid planting species that require constantly wet soil conditions

along the banks and marginal areas of the stream, unless it is a natural swamp or bog, because fluctuations of moisture according to the weather and water flow will mean that these plantings require additional watering. One method of landscaping the edge of a stream is to clear the banks of weeds and to allow plants to appear naturally (still removing weeds as necessary) until an edging garden is well established. Plants that are best suited to the available growing conditions will thrive, and will require little or no ongoing maintenance.

Many of the best-loved water plants, such as waterlilies and lotus, dislike the moving water of a stream, and are therefore best kept for the more tranquil environment of a pond or pool. Instead, look for plants that can be established along the edges of the stream, where water movement will not dislodge their root systems. If the stream divides the property a bridge may be required, allowing the beauty of the scene to be enjoyed from both sides. Alternatively, in a shallow stream, large stepping stones placed closely together for comfortable walking will serve the same purpose.

A Woodland Stream

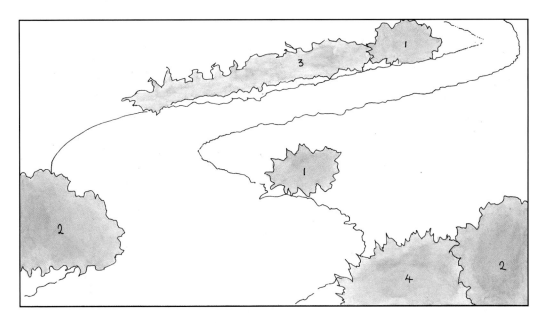

Key to Planting Plan

1. *Digital* sp. (Foxgloves) H. 5 feet
2. *Rhododenron* 'Elizabeth' H. 6 ¹/₂ feet
3. *Hedera helix* (Ivy)
4. *Juniperus procumbens* H. 30 inches,
S. 3 ¹/₄ feet

H. = Height
S. = Spread

A meandering stream or brook gives the opportunity for creative planting, especially on the margins and banks. Streams that have a natural flow of water will not be suited to deep water plants such as waterlilies, because the movement of water will dislodge them. Instead concentrate on accent plants such as foxgloves (*Digitalis* sp.) and rhododendrons, which enjoy the moist soil conditions providing there is adequate drainage. Here ivy (*Hedera helix*) has been allowed to spread as a ground cover, helping to hold the banks together, and the spreading *Juniperus procumbens* overhangs the water, which is always an attractive effect.

A Pebble Pond

Smooth river stones can be employed as a decorative feature in garden pools and ponds, either in the base of the pool or as an edging treatment. This use of pebbles falls short of a completely natural look, although it does combine the natural elements of stone and water. In a 'natural' water garden stones would be used in a much less static or formalistic fashion. However, the tradition of pebble pond landscaping allows for great freedom of expression.

If pebbles are used in a shallow pond —it need only be 3 inches deep—they will glisten and shimmer; only a minimum quantity of water is needed to create an entrancing visual effect. This style of water garden is often incorporated into formal courtyards, which can be either paved or finished with a layer of gravel. No major excavation or plumbing is required—a cost factor that appeals to many landscapers and gardeners.

As a rule, when using rock and stone in general landscaping, one should avoid using different types (such as sandstone and ironstone) because the combination tends to destroy the natural harmony of the garden. However, in a pebble garden this aesthetic rule has less weight as there is no attempt to recreate nature, but instead to highlight the interesting and unusual tones and shapes of the rocks.

In a contemporary courtyard setting a rock or pebble water garden can be used as a design feature and combined with a theme garden, such as one planted with cacti and other succulent plants. Pebbles and stones are an integral part of cacti and desert gardens; and by introducing a shallow pond area where the smooth stones are highlighted by water the garden will be given an added, cooling dimension. Obviously, this style of garden is suited only to warmer climates or to controlled environments such as a large glassed-in courtyard.

When collecting rocks or pebbles, visit a quarry or nursery that stocks construction materials for pools and ponds. Remember that river stones are a natural resource that should be left where they are in wild streams; to remove them will eventually disturb the natural balance of the environment.

OPPOSITE: Here different types of rock have been combined. The small, circular patio pond is surrounded by a collection of smooth river stones, which glisten when splashed by water. Several larger boulders have been used for accent, and their weathered appearance makes a pleasing contrast.

A Pebble Pond

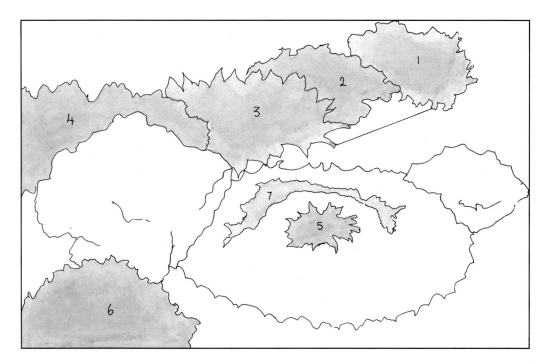

Key to Planting Plan

1. *Dianthus plumarius* (Pinks) H. 20 inches
2. *Erigeron karvinskianus* H. 1 ¹/₂ feet
3. *Hosta sieboldii* (Plantain lily) H. 2 ¹/₂ feet
4. *Anemone nemorosa* H. 6 inches
5. *Butomus umbellatus* (Flowering rush)
H. 4 ¹/₂ feet
6. *Rhododendron kaempferi* H. 8 feet
9. *Azolla caroliniana*

H. = Height

Surrounded by a frame of smooth river stones, this small pond is the main feature of a paved area of the garden. The plants have been used in this stylized plan to add softness, and include azaleas, dianthus and erigeron, and the dramatic foliage plant *Hosta sieboldii*.
In the water the rush (*Butomus umbellatus)* forms an attractive clump, and the water surface is partially covered by the floating *Azolla caroliniana.* In small ponds avoid overcrowding with waterplants, which will deplete the water of oxygen and compete for nutrients.

A Japanese Water Garden

Of all the exotic landscaping styles admired in the West, the Japanese garden is probably the most popular. It is a style that has been imitated by European gardeners since 1868, when Japan was first opened up to the Western world after the Meiji restoration. Certain botanists of the day believed that the Japanese hated plants, because of their habit of 'torturing' them (bonsai); however, there has since emerged an understanding of the true nature of Japanese gardens and gardeners, and their intrinsic worship of nature.

Water is an essential element in the design of a Japanese garden. The use of rocks and stones, even enormous boulders, is also a continual theme and in some locations large cranes are required to move boulders into place to gain the desired effect. Stones placed beside fresh water must be those found naturally in that setting, not rocks of mountain or seaside origin. In essence the Japanese garden is very simple, very subtle; however, a great deal of time and trouble (and money) may be spent to achieve this low-

key effect. The placement of rocks, in particular, is quite intricate, and landscape designers who concentrate on Japanese-style gardens may spend days or even weeks moving rocks around until exactly the right balance and harmony have been achieved.

Purists are quite strict about Japanese landscaping, stressing the subtlety and spirituality of the design. Nevertheless, you should feel free to attempt to capture some of the mood and atmosphere of an oriental water garden in your own landscape. Keep in mind, however, that simply putting a small concrete lantern on the edge of the pond does not create an instant Japanese garden. Consider other aspects such as the use of rocks and stone, the choice of plant material and, most importantly, the scale of the garden. In many ways a Japanese garden is a microcosm of nature; a scaled-down version of a pond or pool that could be found in the wilderness. It is this feeling that must be recreated for the garden to be successful.

Form and texture are integral to the design of a Japanese garden. Rocks are

OPPOSITE: Inspired by the harmony and peacefulness of Japanese landscape design, this water garden uses rocks and stone lanterns to create an oriental atmosphere. Water gently cascades over flat rocks, from one level to another, while waterlilies hold their beautiful blooms high above the water.

naturally weathered, covered in mosses and lichen, and pottery water jars, usually filled by a delicate trickle of water from a spout of bamboo, also need to have a patina of age. The idea is to make the garden appear as though it has always been there; not contrived or planned in any way.

Brightly hued foliage and flowers are usually avoided, with the exception of delicate Japanese maples (*Acer palmatum* sp.) which are seen as edging or accent plants near ponds or lakes. These turn a dramatic, deep burnished scarlet or golden yellow in autumn. Other plants commonly used include bamboo (*Bambusa* sp.), cotoneasters, camellias, shapely conifers, red and black pines (*Pinus* sp.), cedars (*Cedrus* sp.), and a variety of rushes and sedges. Waterlilies are grown as deep-water plants, in areas of the garden that receive sufficient sunshine.

Bridges are often seen as a symbol of Japanese garden style, and are used in the West in the most successful oriental gardens. A bridge should be gently arched and of a simple design, linking two areas of the garden rather than standing out as a design feature on its own.

LEFT: A bamboo water spout sends a fine stream of water onto a moss-covered stone. This setting typifies Japanese design in its simplicity and careful and creative use of natural materials.

OPPOSITE: Various elements have been combined effectively to create this Japanese-style water garden. Framed by a bamboo screen, the garden is part of a small internal courtyard. Rocks have been used in a subtle arrangement, and various ornaments have also been used with restraint.

A Japanese Water Garden

Key to Planting Plan

1. Nymphaea 'Rose Arey' S. 6 ¹/₂ feet
2. *Hibiscus rosa-sinensis* 'Orange Pride'
H. 3 ¹/₄ feet
3. *Verbena* x *hybrida* H. 8 inches
4. *Juniperus horizontalis* (Creeping juniper)
H. 20 inches

H. = Height
S. = Spread

Restraint is the way to approach planning and planting a Japanese-style garden. Avoid incorporating all the elements of Japanese design, as the finished effect may be too cluttered. The use of rock is a vital factor, and here two pools are linked by a small flow-stone, with water dripping slowly from the top to the lower level. Plants have been selected for their hues, such as the waterlilies (nymphaea 'Rose Arey'), the hybrid verbena and the attractive hibiscus, *H. rosa-sinensis* 'Orange Pride'. The stone lantern, which is a traditional Japanese accessory, stands alone on the water's edge, framed by plants.

A Formal Water Garden

A formal garden is one in which symmetry and design overpower nature, but is just as appealing to garden lovers as any natural copse or wild woodland. Formal gardens change in style according to fashion, and often elements of various periods in garden history are combined to reflect the taste and individuality of the owner. The term 'formal' covers all the historic water gardens seen throughout Europe, the Middle East, and Great Britain; it is the antithesis of the style of the oriental water garden, in which great pains have been taken to emulate nature in every detail.

When we think of a formal water garden we tend to imagine a rectangular pool and fountain, set in a traditional courtyard or garden with neatly trimmed lawns and formal flower beds. Yet there are many other ways that water can be used in the garden, following the basic concepts of formal design. Cascades, for example, have been constructed on very strict lines in Britain. They include the great cascades at Chatsworth, in Derbyshire, which are built on moors above the house and consist of a series of steps with water flowing over them and into a succession of holding pools. At the top of the cascades is a temple with a remarkable dome-shaped fountain—all very formal and symmetrical in design and execution.

Rills, which are often built along straight and narrow lines, evolved from irrigation channels used in gardens of the Middle East. As a formal alternative to a brook or stream, the rill is an interesting way of moving water through the garden. Rousham House, in Oxfordshire, has a rill known as the Watery Walk which weaves beautifully between the established trees. Canals are formal in design too and have both practical and aesthetic functions.

The ideas found in the majestic European gardens can easily be translated into a modern garden; obviously on a much smaller and more modest scale. (For example, instead of using natural rocks and boulders as the basis of the

OPPOSITE: Formal water gardens can be of any size, from a tiny symmetrical pond to an elaborate large-scale plan such as those seen in the grand landscapes of Europe. On a more modest scale, this charming formal garden is edged and surrounded by weathered stone pavers and Chinese ceramic urns of flowering perennials. A variety of waterlilies has been used, while a central fountain sends out fine jets of water.

water garden, concrete or sandstone blocks can be used to create a formal design.) Most of the early garden designs were formal, and they inspire modern landscapers and designers with the beauty and simplicity of their lines. Gardeners should take an architectural approach, and enjoy a sense of freedom in determining shape or form. Formal pools built *above* ground, for example, can still readily contain the essence of traditional water garden design.

Creating a formal water garden is less complex than the construction of a garden that imitates nature. There is more control and, while technically the construction must be precise, the scope for serious error is less. Once again, scale is important. As gardens have grown smaller so too must the size of the pond, pool, cascade, or waterfall.

ABOVE: A large formal water garden uses raised beds of shrubs and perennials to frame a spacious square pool that is concrete-lined and edged with smooth stone pavers.

OPPOSITE: Eight curved jets of water emerge from a simple spout, making air bubbles as they hit the water's surface.

A Formal Water Garden

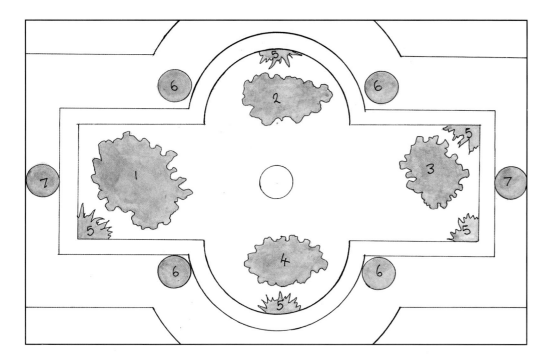

Key to Planting Plan

1. *Nymphaea* 'Gladstoniana' S. 10 feet
2. *Nymphaea* x *laydekeri* S. 3 ¹/₄ feet
3. *Nymphaea* 'Sunrise' S. 8 feet
4. *Nymphaea* 'Rembrant' S. 6 ¹/₂ feet
5. *Iris ensata* H. 2 feet
6. *Phlox caespitosa* H. 4 inches
7. *Abies nordmanniana* 'Gold Spreader'
H. 3 ¹/₄ feet

H. = Height
S. = Spread

A formal garden need not be stark or bland in style, if plants are used with imagination and flare. Here a variety of waterlilies such as nymphaea 'Gladstoniana', *Nymphaea* x *laydekeri,* nymphaea 'Sunrise' and nymphaea 'Rembrandt' have been planted at each end and in the semi-circular curves of the pool, to soften the impact. In the corners, there are clumps of *Iris ensata,* while around the edges, traditional glazed ceramic pots have been arranged symmetrically, planted with phlox and the dwarf conifer *Abies nordmanniana.* The central fountain lightly splashes water into the pool, which helps to keep the water sparkling clean.

THE MAKING
OF A GARDEN

Basic Construction Techniques

In some gardens water occurs naturally, and can be used in developing either a simple or an elaborate water garden. Having a stream running through the garden immediately gives scope for landscaping creativity, and provides an ideal environment for the cultivation of a wide range of wonderful moisture-loving plants. However, most yards are without a natural water source. The introduction of water must be planned and designed, then constructed.

This is not to suggest that the finished garden should be contrived or artificial in appearance. Indeed, some of the most successful gardens have been sculptured from the bare earth, and yet after a few years appear as though they had always been there, formed by Nature's hand. The secret is to position the water within the contours of the land so that the structure of the garden is both feasible and believable.

Of course, many water gardens, including those that are formal or contemporary in design, have no need to emulate nature. These gardens are designed as a feature in themselves; they stand alone, often apart from the landscape. Whatever your choice of style or design, the water garden should be artfully constructed to bring about the pleasure and beauty you desire.

NATURAL WATERCOURSES

Those blessed with a stream at the bottom of the property can do a great deal to enhance the stream's beauty with edging plants and careful landscaping. However, it is important to avoid compromising the natural flow and health of the stream in any way through interference. When water flows from one private property to another it usually means that ownership is shared, and therefore no

PREVIOUS PAGE: The painstaking artistry of creating a water garden on many levels, with elaborately integrated stone and pockets of soil for growing a wide range of conifers, ground covers, and flowering perennials. The water flows gently down over a series of cascades and falls, eventually filling a languid pond.

OPPOSITE: Lush growth is evidence of the health of this small but interesting pond, concrete-lined and edged with locally available stone that has developed a wonderful mossy covering with age. Hostas love poolside growing conditions, especially if the area is partially shaded.

ABOVE: *Planting the surrounds with suitable species, like these lady's mantle (alchemilla) helps to soften the edges and cover any joins in the rockwork that appear artificial. Here the edging rock overhangs, in an attempt to hide the rim where the pool lining is above water.*

individual should change the flow by damming or diverting the stream. In certain situations local water authorities may give permission for changes, but these will need to be monitored by a civil engineer.

Care must be taken to preserve the purity of the water. In the past many waterways have been polluted by chemicals, biological imbalances, and silting, and these are issues that will need to be considered. Avoid the use of pesticides or chemical nutrients in areas where water runoff will flow into the stream. Sewage and animal manures can also be a problem because they may alter the biological balance of the stream, affecting fish and plants and increasing algae growth. The soft earth along the banks of the stream should be cared for to prevent erosion, which can occur after unexpected heavy rain. In the long term it is possible to strengthen the banks by planting various species with roots that help to bind the soil. In the short term the sides of the stream may require reinforcing with crushed rock aggregate, to form a mulch or packing. In some cases larger rocks and rubble may be needed to hold the banks together.

The base of a natural watercourse can be partially lined with river stones or pebbles, crushed quartz, or even limestone. However, if the watercourse is large, importing materials to the site will probably be expensive.

At all times, a natural waterway should be nurtured and protected, as unspoiled waters are such a valuable resource in any community. The ecology of the stream must be preserved, and it is the responsibility of the individual owners to ensure that their section of the stream is well maintained. Avoid the use of plants that will choke or block the stream; only introduce species that will not be invasive or harmful. (See Chapter Five on water plants.)

ARTIFICIAL WATER GARDENS

Compared with a natural watercourse an artificial pond, lake, or stream is a much more controlled and self-contained environment. This allows the gardener true creativity in landscaping, and while the immediate environment must be considered it is not of overriding importance. Perhaps the main issue will be the source of the water, as in times of low rainfall, especially in regions that are prone to lengthy dry periods, lack of water may be a problem. Where moving water is used as a feature, as in a waterfall or babbling stream, the one volume of water should be stored and circulated. However, if the water surface area is large, some will be lost by evaporation. In some gardens underground water may be available, although the quality of this is variable. Tank water collected from the roof may also be used, but in dry weather it may soon dry up. Ideally, large or extravagant water gardens should only be built where there is some permanent source of water.

CHOOSING THE SITE

In nature, water gathers at the base of a slope. This basic fact should be kept in mind if the garden design is to have credibility. On land without a variety of levels, or without slopes, the water garden can probably be located anywhere, positioned more for accessibility and aesthetics than for logic. A simple pond or garden pool is ideal for a small level garden or courtyard, as mixed terrain is required for the movement of water in cascades or a waterfall—unless special construction is undertaken. Streams can also be used, with submersible or hidden pumps used to recirculate the water through the garden. However, where a stream feeds into a pond or pool some variation of height or slope will be necessary.

Obviously, the major purpose of any water garden is to be a dramatic feature of the property, and therefore a site should be chosen that will give the maximum impact. Better still, the stream or pond should be capable of being viewed from several vantage points around the garden, perhaps with some seating or a gazebo located nearby for relaxed enjoyment.

In yards where the land is sloping or of various levels, the location of water gardens must take into account the contours of the land. Pools will always be located where the land is at its lowest, while cascades and waterfalls will be located to merge with the slopes. The pool at the base of the slope is called the 'catchment', while the pool at the top is generally referred to as the 'header'. Just as headwaters initiate the flow of a river, so the header pool serves as the starting point for the waterfall or cascade.

Another important consideration when planning a water garden is its exposure to the sun. Waterlilies (*Nymphaea* sp.) and sacred lotus (*Nelumbo* sp.), like most water plants, must have full sun in order to flower and therefore ponds must be open and in full sun. Ponds shaded by trees, especially deciduous species, will be constantly fouled by falling leaves, bark, and debris, and this must also be taken into account.

CONSTRUCTION MATERIALS

In planning the building of a water garden there are many options in terms of construction materials. The size of the garden will often determine the materials to be used, along with the manual expertise of the person who is doing the installation. While elaborate water gardens will probably require some expert knowledge or guidance, the simpler pond, pool, or waterfall can easily be put together by any gardener.

Concrete

Concrete is one of the most popular materials used in the making of waterways. It is relatively easy to work with and, providing a few basic rules are followed, should cause no problems. The neutral tone of concrete will weather and blend in with the environment and, if well finished and landscaped, the fact that it is artificial will be difficult to notice.

Any pool larger than 10 feet across is considered an ambitious project. It may be beyond the capabilities of the average gardener. From start to finish, the concreting must take no more than about eight hours if it is to be completely waterproof; therefore larger areas will no doubt need a team of people working to finish the job within this period. It is also important that the concrete be well mixed, with the proportions of cement and other ingredients properly balanced, to get the best results. Poorly measured and mixed concrete will split and crack, causing water seepage at the base and sides of the pond or stream.

The area to be excavated must be stable and dry to perform as a solid foundation for the concrete. The depth of the pond is important for two reasons: a) many water plants will not grow in very deep water, and the planting will be limited to those that will grow around the edges; b) there are often local restrictions on the depth of pools and ponds, for safety reasons. In some areas any body of water deeper than 1 foot is considered a 'swimming pool' and may need to be enclosed with safety fencing.

The basic steps for building a pool are:
1. Excavate a smooth firm hole, making sure that it is not too deep and that the sides are not too steep (without formwork the concrete will slide from the sides).
2. Line the hole with 2 inches of builder's sand, packing it down well and smoothing the surface to form an even foundation.
3. Cover the sand with black plastic sheeting that will act as a waterproof membrane. The plastic also helps the concrete to cure more evenly, because moisture is not absorbed from the freshly poured concrete into the sand layer.
4. Even small ponds require some wire reinforcement to strengthen the concrete lining. Chicken wire laid over the plastic membrane is sufficient in a small to medium-size pond; larger pools need a heavy metal mesh that has been cut to fit in sections. The wire or mesh should not be directly in contact with the plastic. It can be lifted above the plastic by placing a few small rocks underneath that will elevate it about 2 inches .
5. The concrete, a mixture of 2 parts sand, 1 part cement, and 3 parts coarse aggregate, should be of an even consistency that is neither too thick nor too runny. When pouring, the concrete should flow easily through the wire or mesh so that it makes full contact with the plastic below. However, if it is too sloppy it will slide down the sides when this area is being constructed. Use a slender piece of wood to push the concrete through the mesh, as 100 percent contact is important. The finished depth of the concrete should be 4 inches, which means that it will be 2 inches above and below the reinforcing mesh.

A handy tip: place some scaffolding, such as wooden painting planks, over the pool for easy access when pouring, thus avoiding the need to walk on the plastic or reinforcing mesh.
6. Keep the mixing and pouring of the concrete a smooth and continuous production, whether using a wheelbarrow or a small concrete mixer. If one area of concrete partially dries it will not knit together well with the next pouring, and this will create weak joins that may leak.

OPPOSITE: Two different types of rock have been combined with surprising success. At the back of the pond weathered stone has been layered to form a small rockery and waterfall, interplanted with a variety of perennials and ground covers. At the front, smooth paving stones overhang the edge, hiding the concrete lining.

7. Smooth the concrete surface with a trowel in successive sections while it is still workable. Remember that the concrete will dry rapidly, leaving a messy finish.

8. The concrete needs to cure well to give it additional strength. It can be filled with water as soon as the surface dries and this will slow down the curing process, giving extra strength. The pond may need to be filled and emptied twice to leach out the surface cement which would make the water alkaline (and unsuitable for fish and most plants). Chemical curing, which involves washing the surface with hydrochloric acid to neutralize the shell, is less wasteful of water, but care must be taken to avoid inhaling the fumes or allowing the acid to come into contact with skin, eyes, or clothing.

9. Some gardeners are happy to leave the concrete to weather naturally, but there are various finishing treatments that are sometimes used:

a) Incorporating stones or aggregate: this is done to give the concrete surface a more natural appearance, and is very useful in shallow streams to give a bubbling effect as the water moves across the stones. The material will need to be placed on the concrete surface while it is still moist, and pressed down firmly. A mixture of stones and gravel of various sizes will help to give a more natural finish.

b) Rendering or bagging: this will give a rougher, more natural finish to the concrete surface, especially if the render is mixed with sand or fine gravel. Most renders are a mixture of sand and cement, and special powders of various hues can be mixed in to create a specific effect. A waterproofing agent can also be incorporated to help seal the surface.

Bricks

Bricks are an excellent material for the construction of formal above-ground or in-ground pools, where the shape is to be either square or rectangular. The straight sides of the pool are easily formed with brickwork, a task that is difficult using concrete as formwork is required for support while the concrete dries.

In most cases the base of the pond will be a reinforced concrete slab 4 inches thick, slightly thicker around the edge of the slab because this will be the foundation for the brickwork. This foundation obviously must be level and smooth. It must incorporate upright metal rods, spaced between 12 inches and 16 inches apart, to bind the concrete base and brick walls together. Depending on the size of the pond, the walls can be either single or double brick—in general above-ground pools are double brick, while those set into the ground need only to be single brick.

If you use concrete blocks instead of bricks lay them so that the holes are vertical, filling them progressively with a mixture of sand and cement.

Rubber or plastic (PVC) lining

The easiest pool construction for the average home gardener is the lined pool, which requires few building or landscaping skills. The improved quality of lining materials means that these pools can now be built to last for decades, and even very large ponds can be attempted because the liners are wide

ABOVE: Even with a small pond the smooth laying of the concrete is important, and should be done as quickly as possible to avoid any seams or joins. Here the shallow hole has been excavated, and a bed of sand laid as a foundation.

enough to be laid in a single sheet. Previously, thick black plastic sheeting was used, but there are several grades of two-ply rubber sheeting which are resistant to aging, weathering, and chemicals. They are unaffected by ultraviolet light, and are easy to repair should they spring a leak.

Excavation and preparation of the hole are important, because a smooth surface will prevent holes being made in the liner. Remove all stones, rocks, and

ABOVE: Before adding fish or plants, the concrete must be leached of lime by filling the pond with water and emptying it several times over. Weathered rocks soften the edges of this small pond, which nestles beside a gravel walkway through the sheltered courtyard.

rubble from the base and sides of the pool, and line it with a 2 inch layer of firmly packed builder's sand or wet newspapers. Drape the PVC or rubber liner over the hole so that it conforms approximately to the shape of the pool. Fold the corners over and remove any excess liner with a sharp razor or scissors. Although there will be wrinkles in the pool, as it slowly fills with water these will disappear.

When the pond has been filled the top edge of the liner will need to be anchored and hidden from sight. This is done by carefully excavating a trench around the edge of the pool and burying the liner beneath a layer of soil. Rocks and stones can then be used to edge the pool, interplanted with species that like moist growing conditions (see Chapters Five and Seven).

Prefabricated fiberglass

Small to medium-size ponds, waterfalls, and cascades are available in kit form, with prefabricated units that fit together in a modular fashion. The appearance of these pool units has improved over the years. They are light and easy to handle, and are finished in a roughcast sandy surface that has a natural texture.

When digging a hole for the prefabricated pool, ensure that there is a good match in size and shape. The hole should be free from rocks or other sharp objects, and lined with 2 inches of builder's sand to cushion the weight of the pool. Simply position the pool, making sure it is well supported on all sides, then fill it slowly. Bring the soil back to the edge of the pool, and finish off with rocks and plants for a softening effect.

POOLSIDE LANDSCAPING

The Surroundings

Once the basic construction of your water garden has been completed, the task of making it beautiful begins. While the water is a wonderful attraction in itself, especially moving, swirling water, the immediate surroundings should be planned and landscaped to enhance it. First of all, before plants can be selected and established, stones or rocks need to be positioned and any pathways or bridge-work completed.

VIEWS

Water always attracts the eye. The surroundings should be designed so that views of the water garden are possible from several different vantage points. This can be achieved by creating walkways or paths or spanning the waterway with a bridge. Middle distance views are the most rewarding; a gazebo, pavilion, pergola, or outdoor living area located a small distance from the water will allow it to be viewed in relation to the entire surrounding landscape. Closer up, a small jetty or deck will provide contact with the water and a place to observe fish and plants at close range.

REFLECTIONS

The play of light on the surface of water brings a magical quality to the garden. This can be intensified by the positioning of striking trees, shrubs, and waterside plants that will be mirrored in the water. Even small ponds will reflect light unless they are crowded with plants, and this may determine what is set nearby. On large ponds or lakes, glare from the water may be a problem in summer. Trees and shrubs can be used to screen the glare from water seen from a nearby house or outdoor living area.

ROCKS AND STONES

Rocks and water are perfect partners; they always work together beautifully in the landscape. When artificial ponds, waterfalls, or streams are installed, the use of rocks to landscape the surrounds will promote a harmonious relationship. The sight and sound of water skipping over pebbles, or cascading over stone

OPPOSITE: Here a winding brick pathway allows the beauty of the water garden to be enjoyed from many vantage points. Between the path and the water are wide beds of perennials, while rushes arch gracefully over the water's edge.

PREVIOUS PAGE: A pretty perennial bed filled with primroses, poppies, and ranunculus provides a bright backdrop to a fern-edged pool. There is great potential for adventurous planting around water; remember that the plants will be reflected in the water's surface.

waterfalls, will give the garden great character and appeal.

In many respects, it is preferable to use stone from your local area when landscaping. For practical reasons it should be less expensive and more accessible. Visually, it will blend in better with the immediate environment and be more 'at home' than imported stone. Never remove rocks from wilderness areas, parks, or wild rivers or streams, as this is regarded as an act of vandalism in most countries. If every gardener were to dip into these natural resources, our wild places would soon be depleted. Fortunately, in many gardens rocks occur naturally, sometimes buried just beneath the surface, and they can be lifted and used for building rockeries or for landscaping pool surrounds. Excavated rocks such as these lack the weathered appearance of moss or lichen, which will take several years to develop.

Most stone used for landscaping has been cleared from fields by farmers, and can be bought directly from them or through a specialist landscape supplier. It is not, however, an endless resource, and must always be used with great care. Avoid mixing different types of rock—for example, sandstone, basalt, or volcanic—as this is contrary to the laws of nature and will destroy the harmony of the garden. Choose rocks that are solid and undamaged, with interesting shapes that will work within the scale of your garden.

Although the addition of rocks can be one of the later stages of landscaping around a water garden, it should be planned in advance. Indeed, in many gardens large rocks will form a major design function, such as a large upright rock used as the 'fall' for a waterfall or the imposing boulders that frame the sides of a cascade. Here the rocks need to be selected with great care, and moved on to the site during the construction stage.

Moving large rocks is a physical challenge, unless you have a huge team of workers such as those used to build the pyramids of Egypt. Rocks of impressive size may need to be lifted into place by a small crane or bulldozer, and positioned with care so that they do not shift and roll out of place. Smaller boulders may still need two or three people to shift them, using crowbars and blocks of wood as a fulcrum. They should be shifted very slowly, a few inches at a time, and settled once in place by jamming smaller stones and rubble under their sides to prevent them from moving. To save back-breaking effort always work out in advance, on a simple plan or sketch, exactly where each boulder is to be placed, and which way up it will face. Shifting boulders from one spot to another is a lot more difficult than rearranging the furniture, so be prepared before the serious work begins!

Some stones look best when laid flat on their sides, while others are more effective placed vertically. For example,

RIGHT: There are many ways that rocks can be used effectively: as edgings, cascades, waterfalls; or to divide the waterway into various sections for different fish and plants. Moisture-loving plants thrive in the boggy soil conditions between the rocks.

ABOVE: Moving rocks of considerable size requires skill, and in some cases a bulldozer or crane may be required. Brilliant yellow yarrow (Achillea sp.) highlights this simple pool, where rocks have been laid at interesting angles, sometimes on their sides.

level. Instead of just edging the pool, the rocks can be allowed to spill into the water, half submerged, for a more interesting effect. This will also provide some stability for marginal plants, helping to keep the submerged planting soil from drifting away.

To help age the rocks and give them a weathered appearance, smother them with fresh animal manure and sprinkle with dried spores from moss. The humid conditions found at the edge of the pond will hasten the process of germination.

BRIDGES

A small bridge spanning a stream is surely one of the most charming additions to any garden. The arched bridges of ancient China which make, by reflection in the water, a complete circle, are justly admired by garden lovers everywhere. However, bridges should be both functional as well as beautiful in concept and design. They should be placed in the landscape for reasons over and above decoration. There should always be a good reason why a bridge is located in a particular spot—presumably to provide access from one side of the stream or pond to the other! Too often oriental arched bridges are put in a garden just for effect, and have a tendency to look greatly contrived. Although normally designed to span water, bridges can be used in undulating gardens to span dips in the ground or to level out pathways, and in fact are more justified in these cases than when used purely for decoration.

Ideally, a bridge should be positioned at the narrowest point between the banks of a stream or pond, and these banks

flat rocks on the water's edge will make a pool appear wider and more generous. Vertically placed rocks are good for falling water, and give height to a waterfall. In general, rocks should be placed as they would be found in nature. For this reason, the use of too many of a similar size or shape will appear unnatural, especially if they are used symmetrically as an edging. Mix different sizes and shapes, layering and overlapping them. Avoid the use of mortar to hold the rocks

in place; instead pack underneath them with rubble and smaller stones to secure their position. Test the rocks well to make sure they will not shift by watering around them and packing in more rubble if necessary.

One of the major uses of stonework will be in the edging of the pool or pond, to link it with the surrounding landscape. Stone will effectively disguise a concrete or rubber pool lining, which will look unnatural rising above water

ABOVE: A simple yet sturdy timber bridge spans a Japanese-style water garden. Since it is close to the water, railings are unnecessary, and the planks are wide enough for comfortable single-file walking. The mature carp can be fed from the bridge, where they gather in lively anticipation.

should be level on either side—for ease of construction. Spanning streams should provide few problems but a pond may be too wide to accommodate a bridge comfortably, unless the pond consists of two water areas with a narrow section in the middle. If the bridge is to be used frequently it must be wide enough to cross comfortably—at least 4 1/2 feet—for two people walking side by side. A narrow bridge of 2 feet can be negotiated, but it is a bit like walking the plank. Handrails may be required, for safety as much as anything, to prevent people slipping on wet surfaces and to stop small children from plunging into the water.

The building materials used will be determined by the style of garden, the expertise of the bridge builder, and the budget allowed. Traditional stone bridges, gently arched to span the water, are among the most beautiful, but require expert building skills. Structurally, the bridge will need strong abutments, which are the equivalent of foundations in that they support both ends of the bridge and absorb the horizontal load. If the bridge is to span two solid rocks the building of artificial abutments will not be necessary, as the bridge can be anchored to the rock. However, it is more likely that the sides of the bank will be soft, and concrete or wooden piers will have to be sunk into the ground to provide the support. An arched bridge, be it of stone, wood, or concrete, will probably need steps to lead to the arch, and these should have a deep enough tread for comfortable walking.

Wooden bridges, both straight or gently curved, are less expensive and

allow a painted finish, perhaps in the Monet style or the brilliant lacquer red found in Chinese gardens (but only if the style of plantings lends itself to this embellishment). The oriental cantilevered bridge, resembling those seen on old willow-pattern plates, can be constructed from wood; and in a more earthy setting a rustic bridge of weathered logs will always look delightful. Wood should be kept clean and free from dirt which can build up and provide a growing medium for the algae that makes its surface so slippery. Regular sweeping or hosing down will prevent the surface from deteriorating.

Concrete is another choice for bridge building, certainly durable, and appropriate in a contemporary landscape. The bridge can be precast in sections and then put together on the site, supported by sturdy concrete beams.

JETTIES AND DECKING

Large ponds and lakes benefit from a small jetty or pier which, like bridges, can become a place to relax and enjoy the view. In a large lake the pier can be used for boating, although more commonly it is simply a place to sit and dangle your legs over the water, perhaps observing the fish. Piles will need to be sunk underwater as well as on the bank, and if timber is used it must be treated against moisture deterioration. Concrete supports may well be needed to anchor the piles,

LEFT: Larger bodies of water, like this expansive lake, can be enjoyed from a pier. This robust wooden platform makes it easy to get in and out of a rowboat, and is a pleasant place to picnic or to relax in a deckchair.

so expert advice should be sought. Concrete may be used for the entire construction.

Wooden decking around one edge of a pond or lake is another attractive feature, providing easy access to the water. Follow the advice given for bridges for keeping the surface clean and free from algae.

PATHS AND PAVING

For ease of access to your water garden, pathways that are constructed of safe non-slip materials should be incorporated into the landscape. While lawns sweeping down to the water look picturesque they can be treacherous, and an alternative route should be constructed. As in all aspects of garden design, logic should be used when deciding the direction of a path. If there is a bridge, pier, or decking at the pond or lake, the path should lead to and from these points. A curved embankment should be complemented by a curved meandering pathway, perhaps framed on either side with iris or ground-covering plants that will soften the outline of both path and pond. Rustic cobblestones, gravel, or weathered rocks that are smooth enough for safe walking can be used—or concrete, providing it has a finish that does not look harsh or unappealing.

When bricks or clay pavers are used for path construction they should be carefully laid on a thick (2 inch) bed of builder's sand, and then grouted

RIGHT: Comfortable and level walking paths beside the water are an important safety factor. This lush pond is planted with a variety of waterlilies, and edged with dense foliage plants and rambling roses.

ABOVE: This garden has many features to please the eye, from the neatly clipped plants that form topiary sculptures, to the use of stone lanterns as ornamentation. Painted timber archways lead from one area of the garden to another, providing a dramatic contrast to the rich greens of the foliage.

OPPOSITE: A dramatic fluted urn and rather sinister dragon nestled at the back of a lush lily pond in the La Mortola Garden near Ventimiglia in Italy. Unusual fountain designs add visual interest to ponds that are otherwise simple in design.

statuary and fountains; however, they should always be complementary to each other and to the garden as a whole. Avoid mixing classical Italian statues with cute stone replicas of animals and birds or Japanese lanterns—this clash of cultures and styles will destroy the harmony of the setting.

Most water garden nursery specialists have displays of interesting and unusual fountain statuary in concrete, stone, or bronze. They may also sell statuary that, while not piped for water, is suitable for gracing a bank or glade that adjoins the water garden. In formal gardens these features can be centrally located as the main focal point; in more natural gardens they should be positioned in a more subtle way, tucked in a corner where they will provide a sudden visual surprise.

(cemented in between) to prevent weed growth spoiling the finish. There is great opportunity for creativity in the pattern laid, but wise gardeners keep it simple! Paths that adjoin lawns should be set into the ground to avoid the need for edge-trimming, a tedious and time-wasting exercise when the mower can so easily come right up to the edge instead.

FEATURES

There are many decorative features, both simple and elaborate, that can be used to add beauty and charm to a water garden. Restraint is the keyword when introducing ornamentation, as it is easy to obscure the simplicity of natural beauty by too many embellishments. Scale, as always, is an important consideration. In small courtyard gardens with a simple pool, additions such as a wall-mounted fountain or a statue forming part of a waterfall should be understated, never overpowering in size to the other elements of the garden. In larger gardens, be more adventurous in the use of

LIGHTING

If possible a water garden should be lit for nighttime enjoyment. Floodlights can be directed at fountains or waterfalls, catching the movement of the water as dramatically as the sunlight does during the day. Floodlights can also be used to illuminate dramatic poolside plantings, silhouetting the outlines of tree trunks or palm fronds. In formal pools underwater lighting will glow in the evening, creating a wonderful mood and atmosphere in the garden. If the garden is some distance from the house, pathways leading to it will need to be well lit at night, for safety as well as aesthetic reasons. Consult an electrician before installing outdoor or underwater lighting, as there are certain safety requirements that must be observed.

Water
Life

Understanding Water Ecology

The health and ecological balance of the water in your pond, stream, or waterfall should always be taken seriously. Having carefully designed and constructed the water garden you will be disappointed if the water is slimy, smelly, or stagnant, or if it cannot support plant life and fish. For aesthetic reasons the water should be kept as fresh and pure as possible. Although it will probably never be crystal-clear like the treated water in a swimming pool, it can still be sparkling, healthy, and alive.

THE ECOLOGY OF WATER

A healthy pool is one in which the water has attained an ecological balance, so that plants, fish, and other water life work to support each other and thrive. The ecology of each pool, puddle, stream, or rill is different, depending on factors such as its size and shape, the water and air temperature, the position in relation to sun or shade, the amount of oxygen present in the water, whether the water is still or moving, the types of plants used, and the presence of living pond life (fish, snails, frogs, beetles, wasps, worms, flies, etc.). Even in a natural environment, rivers and streams can easily lose their ecological balance in times of drought or heatwave when the water levels drop or streams cease to flow freely. Algae will appear, drastically lowering the oxygen levels in the water and destroying fish, frogs, and other water life. When this occurs on a large scale it is regarded as an environmental disaster; drastic action is required to try to restore the delicate balance.

However, more often than not, it is humans who are the culprits in destroying the ecological balance of water, both in major public waterways and in backyard water gardens. When large amounts of nutrients such as phosphorus or nitrogen enter the water, plant life, especially algae, multiplies and decays, using up the oxygen that is essential for healthy balanced water. Toxic pollutants such as pesticides, chemical fertilizers, and

OPPOSITE: Submerged oxygenating plants help to maintain sound water ecology by reducing algae growth and providing healthy conditions for fish, frogs, and other water life. Moving water contains high levels of oxygen, which is the reason recirculated water gardens are successful.

PREVIOUS PAGE: The health of every water plant, such as these palest pink waterlilies (Nymphaea sp.), is dependent on the health and ecology of the water. The balance of nutrients and oxygen is very important.

petroleum waste can also leach into the water, poisoning pond life. All of these factors contribute to the degradation of our waterways, and on a smaller scale are the reason why many water gardens fail to give pleasure to their owners. By understanding how water can be kept alive we stand a better chance of keeping plants and pond life healthy.

KEEPING THE WATER HEALTHY

Healthy water contains sufficient oxygen to support animal and plant life, and there are various ways by which the oxygen level is kept in balance. Using a process called photosynthesis, plants take in carbon dioxide from the atmosphere and release oxygen back into the atmosphere; or, in the case of water plants, back into the water. Therefore a pond that contains plant life will be rich in oxygen, especially if stocked with 'oxygenating species' that are particularly efficient at the task (see Chapter Six). However, if there are too many plants they will choke the pond, and as their leaves die they will create an oversupply of decaying matter

RIGHT: The surface area of the lilypads keeps the water shady and cool, which in turn helps to keep algae down. If debris from surrounding shrubs and trees falls into the pond it can cause problems as the organic matter breaks down underwater.

OPPOSITE: In a small pond where the water is still, there is always a danger of stagnation. Oxygenating plants and fish help to maintain a balance, while an occasional flushing out of the water with a hose is useful during hot days when algae growth can quickly escalate.

which, as it sinks to the bottom, will use up valuable oxygen through decomposition. Similarly, while fish are good for keeping the pond clean of debris and for cutting down on mosquitoes by eating their larvae, too many fish will also deplete the pond of oxygen, therefore overstocking is ill-advised. Likewise, overfeeding of fish will add nutrients and debris to the water, again breaking down the ecological balance. It is a delicate juggling act: deciding how many and what species of plants; how many and what species of fish.

Here are some helpful guidelines for maintaining healthy water life:

1. Avoid the use of pesticides, herbicides, chemical fertilizers, or rich animal manures in parts of the garden that run off into ponds or pools after rainfall or when the garden is watered.

2. Ensure that stormwater, which may contain harmful pollutants and heavy metals, and sewage do not run off into the water. In light sandy soils, septic tanks can leach into nearby waterways, causing many problems.

3. Avoid overstocking ponds with fish, and overfeeding fish. Also, if fish are in the pool, tap water that has chlorine or chloramine in it cannot be used without the addition of chemicals to neutralize the chlorine.

4. Try to introduce some water movement with a pump or small fountain. Moving water has a greatly increased oxygen content, as does water that is rippled on the surface by wind or splashed by fountains or waterfalls. Try to prevent the water from becoming static or stagnant, especially during periods of hot weather, as algae growth will multiply. In a still pond or pool a hose can be used to flush out debris or pollutants periodically, providing the water from the tap is not a vastly different temperature from that in the pond. Also, if fish are in the pool, tap water that has chlorine or chloramine in it cannot be used without the addition of chemicals to neutralize the chlorine.

5. Test the pH level of the water in a still pond or pool every few months (kits are available from water garden nurseries). The water can become acidic if there is an excess of rotting vegetation, manure (from planting waterlilies), or fish food. Most plants prefer a neutral pH of between 6.8 and 7.6, so maintaining this balance is important. A simple remedy, like a sprinkling of Epsom salts, may be enough to restore the pH level.

6. Cover the pond in the fall if deciduous trees are nearby, as too many leaves will increase the decaying matter in the water, thus reducing the oxygen levels once again.

7. In cold climates where the water freezes over in winter, try to keep one patch free of ice so that gases can escape. When ponds are frozen for long periods, a buildup of gases can destroy all plant and fish life in the water.

8. Regularly monitor the pond for algae growth and any buildup of organic debris or plants. It is far better to prevent a problem early, before fish and other water life are adversely affected.

WATER FILTERING

Some water gardens are designed just for keeping fish, and therefore some filtering process will be required to keep the water pure. Even in ponds that are stocked with oxygenating plants as well as fish, filters are sometimes used for increased water clarity, especially pools that are integrated into houses or public buildings. In smaller pools a portable electric filter can be used to keep the water looking fresh and clean, by filtering out solids and algae. This filter may not need to be run 24 hours a day, but for just a few hours regularly, like a swimming pool filter.

In large water gardens a permanent biological filtering system can be installed, using sand or graded gravel to remove unwanted particles from the water. A pump is needed to take water from the bottom of the pool into the filter. After being filtered it flows back in to the pond near the water surface, via an inflow pipe. During this process the water is naturally aerated as well as filtered, and this makes it ideal for supporting a higher than usual number of healthy fish. A biological filter uses living bacteria in the sand or gravel filtering medium to convert unhealthy nitrates and ammonia, that multiply in the pond, into nitrates that feed plant life. The filter needs to be working constantly, processing the water completely every few hours, to keep the bacteria alive and doing their work.

OPPOSITE: Moving water, like that streaming from the mouth of the classic lionhead fountain, remains fresh and well oxygenated. Even a simple recirculation system helps to keep the water pure, as well as providing all those soothing sounds that make a water garden so enjoyable.

WATER RECIRCULATION

Moving water is preferable because it contains more oxygen; a pond that has a recirculating water system will remain cleaner and support healthier plant and fish life. Pumping water prevents temperature stratification by evenly distributing the water temperature and the oxygen mix. Even small fountains or sprays will help to keep the water fresh, as they bubble and splash, taking in oxygen while the water is circulated.

Electric pumps are used to recirculate water in small artificial streams, waterfalls, and in most fountains. The size, voltage, and horsepower of the pump will be determined by the size of the water garden and the volume of water to be moved. Small, trickling fountains will require only a very small pump; gushing streams and waterfalls may need quite substantial pumps to perform the task. Recirculated water must be filtered before entering the pump, and this also helps to keep the system clean and ecologically balanced by effectively removing algae and other particles.

Modern plumbing methods, using lightweight PVC pipes, have simplified the installation of recirculation systems to the point where the average handyperson can set up a simple fountain or waterfall without professional assistance.

RIGHT: A natural stream system which uses only a small quantity of water that is continuously recirculated from the base of the stream to a simple cascade that is slightly elevated. A system like this uses a small electric pump, which is inexpensive to run.

ABOVE: On a grand scale, a series of waterfalls cascade to form an unusual modern timber log waterfall in Texas. The large pond at the base of the falls is ideal for keeping fish, because of the clarity of the moving water.

WATER
PLANTS

Use of Plants in Water Gardens

A great joy in having a pond or pool in the garden is the possibility of growing all those plants that thrive in or around water, or in moisture-laden soils. As with any landscaping, it is important to understand the growth habit and requirements of each species to be introduced, to ensure that they fulfill your expectations and their own potential. This is particularly true of water plants, because some species are very vigorous growers and can quickly overrun or choke the pond, requiring drastic action to control them.

Different plants are suited to different parts of the pond and its surroundings, and have different functions or uses within the ecology of the water and the immediate setting. There are plants that can be grown in deep water, with roots

OPPOSITE: The creation of a bog garden, like this English woodland garden at Exbury, Hampshire, is a wonderful way of growing a wide range of plants that like wet feet, while making good use of a swampy area of the property. Here ferns, hostas, and azaleas thrive in the moist shade.

PREVIOUS PAGE: At the edge of the pond, iris and hostas thrive in the moisture-laden soil conditions that this setting provides. Massed plantings of one or two species always have a dramatic effect, and they make the garden appear larger.

that travel down to the soil in the base of the pool or into containers filled with a rich growing medium; there are floating plants for deep water that have roots and foliage on, or just beneath, the water surface; there are oxygenating plants that help maintain a healthy ecology within the pond; there are marginal or bog plants that thrive on the water's edge; and there are many species that love the humid microclimate found at the edge of the water.

When looking for suitable plants to landscape your pond first establish what effect is wanted, then find the plants that are best for the purpose. The selection of plants, and how they are arranged, will be determined by more than the climate and the position in relation to sun and shade (although these are obviously important considerations). The style of water garden will also play a vital role in determining which plants are used and how they are grouped together.

In a formal garden, where water is a feature, sculptural trees and shrubs, topiary, and formal container arrangements are appropriate. In an informal water garden the emphasis is on recreating nature, so plants must be selected according to their ability to blend into the environment. In an oriental water garden, plants with a weeping habit (especially maples) are often used to capture the right atmosphere. It helps to study established water

gardens when deciding what style you wish to create, and therefore which plants are best suited to the purpose.

Professional landscapers always draw an initial ground plan that includes a list of suitable species. Research and preparation are just as necessary for the enthusiastic home gardener. Use graph paper to draw a simple outline of the pool, stream, or waterfall, showing where it is located in relation to the entire water garden area and surroundings (the house and other buildings can be shown on the graph paper, drawn to scale). Then pencil in the preferred plants, starting with trees and larger shrubs, and working down to edging plants, marginal plants, and deep-water plants. Be realistic about the size of the garden and the pond, and the scope for growth, so that plants are not chosen that will rapidly outgrow the site and overwhelm the scale of the garden. Most reference books list the mature height and spread of individual plants, and this is a good guideline; however, remember that in warm climates plants will sometimes reach a larger size than in colder regions. Also keep in mind that large spreading trees will eventually take the sun from the garden, which will prevent a great many other species from growing (waterlilies *must* have the sun in order to flower). Also consider the problem of

ABOVE: Irises like the growing conditions on the margins of the pond, although they can also be grown in garden beds if well watered. They are available in a spectacular range of hues, and do best in temperate, warm, or tropical regions.

deciduous trees dropping their leaves into the water, which can dirty it and upset the ecological balance.

The same basic ground rules apply as for planning and planting any part of the garden. Of course it is very tempting to buy more plants than are actually required, but through overplanting and overcrowding certain species will probably fail to thrive or will become diseased. It is sometimes hard to resist buying plants, especially when they are in flower and look so enchanting, but always stop and consider whether there is really enough space for more plants to be squeezed in. If in doubt, resist!

In positioning plants around a pool or pond, or framing a stream or waterfall, follow the same basic principles used for planting beds and borders. To be seen and admired to their best advantage, plants must be positioned according to height, spread, foliage, hue, texture, and flowering quality and bloom time. Larger growing plants are best placed in the background, gradually reducing in size toward the front of the garden or the edge of the pool. One or two large clumps of taller species can be positioned on the edge as an accent or feature, as long as they do not block the light for other, smaller growing plants.

Discovering how to group plants effectively takes years of gardening experience and practice, although many happy accidents can occur as plants nestle together and complement each other. There are no strict rules in how plants are combined; it is really just a question of individual taste. For some gardeners bright hues that boldly leap out at you have the required impact. Others prefer more subtle shades, pastels and creams, for a softer effect. Then there are theme gardens, where one or two hues predominate: white on green; pink and lilac. Keep in mind that mistakes can always be corrected. In winter plants can be moved around into new positions and even the most experienced gardeners do this all the time, to try to improve the balance and harmony of each area of the garden.

Plants for the water garden are divided into groups, according to where they are planted.

DEEP-WATER PLANTS

These plants have their roots in soil, either at the base of the pond or in containers that are fully submerged. The most commonly grown deep-water plant is the waterlily (Nymphaea sp.), because of its spectacular scented flowers, attractive circular floating leaves, and ease of cultivation. The large leaves, in fact, are quite useful because they shade the water and therefore reduce the algae growth that can use up all the oxygen. They are very good plants for fish ponds, although there is always the problem of fish churning up the soil unless its surface is covered with a thick layer of pebbles or gravel. This applies both to lilies grown at the base of the pool and those planted in submerged containers.

Tropical waterlilies are suited to temperate, sub-tropical, and tropical climates, and require a moderately warm water temperature to survive. Hardy varieties, however, can grow in cool to cold regions, surviving even quite harsh winters. The flowers of most popular

ABOVE: Waterlilies (Nymphaea sp.) *are deep-water plants with roots that must either be planted in the soil at the base of the pond or be in a container that is fully submerged. There are hardy and tropical varieties in a tremendous range of hues from pure white through to deepest red or brilliant yellow.*

varieties are hybrids with double petals. There are miniature varieties for small pools as well as very vigorous growers for large ponds and lakes. The depth of water needed for waterlilies depends on the size of the variety being grown; obviously the depth must be no greater than the length of the foliage stems or the plants will be submerged!

Waterlilies are quite heavy feeders and must be planted in soil that is rich in nutrients. Most specialist nurseries recommend a mixture of 70 percent good quality loam and 30 percent well-aged cow manure, for both container and bottom-planted specimens. Feeding the lilies can be a problem because excess nutrients are not good for the water ecology, and yet the plants must get a boost every year. Try placing a handful of bonemeal in a strong paper bag, then burying it in the soil under the gravel layer. The bag will take a while to break down, slowly releasing the nutrient to the roots.

Other worthwhile deep-water plants include the pretty water poppy (Hydrocleys nymphoides), which has floating leaves and yellow poppy-like flowers held above the foliage; the fragrant cape pondweed (Aponogeton distachyus), which

ABOVE: Caltha palustris '*Flora plena*' is a semi-evergreen perennial with glossy deep green foliage and clusters of bright yellow double flowers which appear in spring. Calthas should be planted in marginal soil at the edge of the pond.

flowers over many months from late winter until the end of summer; the perennial parrot's feather (*Myriophyllum aquaticum*), which has blue-green foliage that is partially submerged; and the vigorous *Nuphar luteum*, which has leathery foliage and unusual, small yellow flowers.

MARGINAL PLANTS

These plants need their root systems to be held in moist boggy soil, either in shallow water or at the edge of the pond. This is the largest group of water plants, and there are many to choose from to soften the edges and embankments of streams and garden pools. Most species are perennials. Care must be taken if the stream or pond is dependent on the weather conditions for water supply, as these marginal areas can dry out during summer or when droughts occur.

One of the most popular and easy-to-grow marginal plants is the perennial pickerel rush (*Pontederia cordata*), which has handsome lance-shaped leaves and spikes of attractive blue flowers in summer. A more delicate plant, also in the blue range, is the water forget-me-not (*Myosotis scorpioides*), which has pretty, bright green foliage and masses of tiny blue flowers. Another species with pretty flowers is brass-buttons, an evergreen with fleshy stems and button-like bright yellow flowers from the beginning of spring to the end of autumn.

In warmer climates the enormous lotus (*Nelumbo lutea*) can be used as a marginal planting, with dramatic foliage and showy yellow flowers in summer.

The Australian variety of sacred lotus (*N. nucifera*) is also suited only to warm regions, and produces wonderful seed capsules that are almost as attractive as the flowers.

The deciduous *Ranunculus lingua* is a useful species, with glossy lance-shaped leaves and yellow flowers in clusters at the end of spring. Various iris are suited to marginal plantings too, including the blue flag iris (*Iris laevigata*) which has mid-green foliage and blue, white, or red flowers, and the yellow flag iris (*I. pseudacorus*) which has silvery green leaves and golden yellow flowers in early spring. Also in the yellow range is the startling marsh marigold (*Caltha palustris*), which has deep green rounded leaves and clusters of bright yellow cup-shaped flowers in spring.

ABOVE: Euphorbia will give a dramatic flower display if planted in a semi-shaded bed that is moist but has good drainage. Euphorbias have similar requirements to many perennials that like rich moist soil, and are frequently planted adjacent to streams or garden pools.

OXYGENATING PLANTS

There are various species that are useful because they add oxygen to the water, which helps to maintain a healthy environment for fish as well as other plants. They grow at the bottom of the pool and compete with algae for light and food; they also use up some of the carbon dioxide exhaled by the fish, converting it into oxygen by the process of photosynthesis. In general these plants are vigorous and will spread quickly, so precautions must be taken to ensure that they do not choke other plant life. Regular reduction of oxygenating plants will prevent this problem.

One of the best known plants in this group is *Azolla caroliniana,* a deciduous perennial used to reduce algae in the water. The plant can spread vigorously and may need to be controlled each season. Another vigorous grower is *Cabomba caroliniana,* which forms dense clumps of bright green foliage. Eel grass, also known as ribbon weed (*Vallisneria spiralis*), also helps to increase oxygen supplies in the water. It is planted in soil at the base of the pond and initially may need to be weighted down with a small stone until the roots are established.

FLOATING PLANTS

There are several interesting plants that float on the water surface, with roots that do not need to be anchored into soil. Duckweed (*Lemna minor*) is one that is commonly grown in pools and ponds. It is recorded as being one of the smallest flowering plants in cultivation. Its tiny leaves cover the top of the water, and it is quite easy to control because excess plants can simply be scooped up and removed. Water lettuce (*Pistia stratiotes*) is a delightful floating plant that really does resemble a lettuce bobbing about in the water. Fish love it, and lay their eggs in its lower leaves and roots. The beautiful water hyacinth (*Eichhornia crassipes*) is another floating variety, but in some countries with warmer climates it is regarded as a noxious weed because it spreads rapidly and chokes natural waterways. In cooler areas it can be controlled more easily, and is admired for its pale mauve flowers.

*ABOVE: Old-fashioned cranesbill (*Geranium *sp.) likes the rich soil conditions near water, but the soil must be well drained as the plant resents having wet feet. There are many varieties, in a wide range of foliage sizes and flower hues; they look attractive when massed planted or mingled with other perennials.*

MATTING PLANTS

These useful plants can be allowed to develop around the edges of ponds and streams, and will consolidate the soil and hold the banks together. Water clover (*Marsilea* sp.) will root in the soil along stream banks, preventing erosion. Swamp mazus (*Mazus pumilio*) forms a mat 2 inches high, and has light green foliage and pretty blue-purple flowers in spring and summer. Another matting plant worth considering is the whorled water milfoil (*Myriophyllum verticillatum*), a fast-growing evergreen perennial with masses of olive green foliage.

RUSHES AND SEDGES

Also for the edge of the water are all those delightful plants with grass-like foliage, such as reeds, rushes, and sedges. These can provide a wonderful habitat for birds and frogs, and are effective accent plants that also help to bind the soil along embankments. Various members of the *Carex* sp. can be grown in clumps near pools and ponds providing the ground is not waterlogged. Myrtle flag (*Acorus calamus*) will grow in the marginal areas, and there is a variegated form which is particularly pretty with fragrant sword-like leaves edged with cream. Flowering rush (*Butomus umbellatus*) is not a true rush, but has similar foliage and pretty pink flowers in summer. *Eleocharis dulcis* is a very hardy rush for the water's edge. Eelgrass (*Vallisneria spiralis*), while it cannot withstand heavy frosts, can be grown successfully in warmer climates, and forms a large clump of green strap-like foliage.

ABOVE: Primula florindae *can be grown in marginal areas or in the rich peaty soil on the edge of a stream. The showy, bell-like sulphur yellow flowers appear in summer, and form a handsome clump up to 3 feet in height.*

INTRODUCING
FISH

Creating a Healthy Environment for Fish

The sight of swimming fish has long been seen as a calming and relaxing therapy for tense or anxious people—why else are fish tanks so often found in dentists' waiting rooms? The slow and rhythmical movement of fish gliding through water is attractive to the eye and soothing to the soul, which explains why so many garden pools and ponds are stocked with goldfish or carp. Keeping fish can be an absorbing hobby, or just a pleasant adjunct to maintaining a pretty water garden. However, some care is needed if your fish are to survive and thrive in an artificially created water environment.

There are many benefits in keeping fish. They feed on debris and insects such as mosquito larvae, helping to keep the water clean and fresh. The carbon dioxide exhaled by fish helps to provide plants with one of the necessary ingredients for photosynthesis. In turn, the oxygen released by the plants meets the respiration requirements of both animals and plants. So, keeping fish can help to maintain the ecological balance of your pond.

SUITABLE FISH

The selection of fish varieties will depend on the size of the pond. Large fish need space, and can only be kept in pools that are large enough to support them. Ideally, only fish that are native to a particular country should be kept, because environmental damage can occur if introduced species manage to get into natural streams and waterways.

Never release exotic ornamental fish into rivers or streams, and ensure your pool will not overflow into a natural waterway during heavy rain.

Koi carp and goldfish are among the most popular fish varieties kept in domestic garden pools. Both species are very beautiful, and can be bought from aquariums and specialist water garden suppliers in a variety of shimmering hues from black through to red, gold, and silver.

Koi carp grow to a considerable size and are really suited only to larger pools, with sufficient space for them to mature in. As with all fish they will not do well if the pond is overstocked and therefore overcrowded. However, they are extremely sociable and responsive creatures that will answer calls or hand-clapping after a little training. They can bring great pleasure and enjoyment to their owners. Carp do not require much supplementary feeding, unless kept in a pool with filtered water. Otherwise they will survive quite well by living off the natural debris that builds up in the water, with perhaps one feeding a week of specially formulated fish food.

Goldfish are also very entertaining fish, and come in a range of delightful hues, shapes, and sizes. Some of the more exotic varieties, such as fantails and black moors, are rather delicate and may not be suited to an outdoor pond if the conditions are relatively rough—they do better in the controlled environment of an indoor aquarium. However, the more common and hardy varieties will thrive in a garden pond, and multiply happily if the conditions are suitable. They lay their eggs in spring, among the roots of floating plants, and even though many hundreds of small fry may emerge only a few will survive to maturity. (The fish themselves will devour both the eggs and the fry.)

OPPOSITE: A lively pond filled with goldfish and dramatic red waterlilies. Fish need plenty of oxygen in the water and will suffer on hot days if algae growth proliferates. If the pond has still water, splash the surface with water from the hose every day to add oxygen.

PREVIOUS PAGE: The pleasure of keeping fish in a garden pool or lake. Here healthy goldfish slip between the stems of waterlilies (Nymphaea sp.) *and parrot's feather* (Myriophyllum aquaticum), *enjoying the cool waters of a small water garden.*

Trout can be kept successfully in large pools and ponds. They are wonderful to watch when they jump, like enchanting slivers of silver, for the insects above water level—usually in the evening or early morning. There are many other smaller fish that are native to various countries; but these are usually rather shy and not as entertaining or as spectacular to look at as koi carp, goldfish, or trout.

INTRODUCING THE FISH

A sudden change of water temperature can be fatal to fish, so they must be introduced into a new environment quite slowly. Most fish are sold in plastic bags, and these can be lowered into the water for half an hour or so to give the water inside the bag time to adjust to the external water temperature. The same can be done if the fish are in a pail or bucket, although they may need to remain there a bit longer until the temperatures have evened out. Get advice about mixing various fish species, as some varieties will prey upon the others. Avoid overcrowding the pond, and check regularly to see if the fish are healthy and thriving.

Newly constructed concrete ponds must be thoroughly leached of the lime in the concrete before fish can safely be introduced. The concrete can be sealed or the pond filled and drained of water several times until it is clean. Allow a few weeks for water plants to settle and chlorine to dissipate from water before adding the fish.

PROBLEMS

The main problem with keeping fish is poor water quality. Fish must have plenty of oxygen to survive and water that is fouled with debris and rotting leaves, or has an excess of algae growth, will not provide a good living environment. That is not to say that the water must be crystal-clear or filtered. See Chapter Five for ways to balance the ecology of the water, to make it suitable for fish.

The factors that contribute to poor oxygen levels in the water are:
• too many fish, especially large fish, competing for the oxygen supply
• too many plants choking the water, especially large lily pads that smother the entire surface
• too much algae
• an excess of decaying leaves and uneaten fish food
• a sudden increase in water temperature during very hot weather (warm water cannot hold oxygen as well as cool water can).

If the fish are gathering near the water surface, and appear to be gobbling at the top layers in search of oxygen, it is an indication that they are becoming distressed. Start running some fresh water into the pond immediately, spraying and splashing the surface to stir it up and thus add oxygen. At the same time, clear as much debris and decaying rubbish as possible from the water, and thin out the plants. (Water from some public water systems has chlorine. Allow the water to stand for 24 hours before adding to the pond, or add chemicals to neutralize the chlorine if fish are to be put in the water.)

Large birds and small animals, including domestic cats, can have great fun plundering a pond, and will quickly reduce the fish population if the surface area is open and exposed. Overhanging rocks at the edge of the pond will provide some shelter for the fish. Terracotta pipes can be laid horizontally on the bottom as a safe place for the fish to dart to and hide. Some pool owners cover the entire water surface with wire mesh, but this looks very unattractive. Instead, make some tubes of open-mesh wire and submerge them below water level. The fish can swim inside and be protected if birds or cats are attacking.

Pollutants such as garden fertilizers, insecticide spray residues, or sewage will also endanger fish if allowed to get into the water. Try to keep chemical additives of all sorts as far from the pond as possible.

Another danger is overfeeding, which is quite unnecessary in a balanced outdoor pool. Too much fish food can foul the water and reduce the oxygen, as well as making the fish dependent on a constant supply. Feed pond fish only once a week; and then only a light sprinkling that will take the fish two or three minutes to completely devour.

OTHER POND LIFE

A healthy pond can sustain other wildlife such as frogs, tortoises, snails, and small crustaceans. Snails are useful pond cleaners, feeding on algae. Frogs can be noisy but are delightful comical creatures that produce tadpoles, which are enthralling for children to observe. Insects, such as dragonflies, often congregate near water and are a pleasant addition to pond life. Large waterbirds, such as ducks, can wreak havoc in small pools and ponds, and are really suited only to large water gardens or lakes.

ABOVE: *Koi-karp are friendly and easily trained to eat from your hand. They will self-regulate their size according to the size of the pond, and care must be taken not to overstock or some will die.*

PLANT SELECTION LISTS

Plants for Water Gardens

Aconitum x bicolor
MONKSHOOD (fs e)

Compact perennial, growing
to 4 feet with glossy deep green
leaves and hooded violet-blue
or white flowers in summer.
Grows well in rich moist soil.
(Zones 3-7)

Acorus calamus
SWEET FLAG (fs m or b)

A semi-evergreen perennial
for the marginal edges of the
pond, with highly fragrant,

*OPPOSITE: Selecting appropriate plants
is the most interesting aspect of water
gardening. Plants like sedum enjoy the moist
soil conditions adjacent to the pool, while
other plants are positioned either in
deep water, or in the marginal areas around
the waterline.*

*PREVIOUS PAGE: Astilbe is a perennial
which grows well in the moist soil conditions
found at the edge of garden pools. It forms a
large clump of attractive foliage, and in
summer features tall stems of feathery flowers
that vary in hue according to the variety.*

sword-like foliage. There is a
variegated form with green
and cream markings, flushed
with pink in spring.
(Zone 3)

Acorus gramineus variegatus
GRASSY-LEAVED SWEET FLAG (fs m or b)

A semi-evergreen perennial with
grass-like foliage of deep green,
variegated with cream. Grows to
10 inches around the pond margins.
(Zone 5)

Alisma plantago-aquatica
WATER PLANTAIN (fs m)

A semi-evergreen perennial with
delicate bright green foliage
carried above the water, and
small pink or white flowers in
spring. Grows to $3^{1}/_{4}$ feet.
(Zone 5)

Aponogeton distachyus
WATER HAWTHORN, CAPE POND WEED (fs d)

A deciduous or semi-evergreen
perennial with leathery floating
foliage and heavily scented
white flowers with dark stamens;
produced in late winter, spring,
and summer. Grows to $3^{1}/_{2}$ feet.
(Zone 10)

Astilbe
FEATHER FLOWER, GOAT'S BEARD (fs e)

A clump-forming perennial with
glossy dark green foliage and willowy
spikes of small cream/white or pink
flowers during mid-summer. Grows
from $3^{1}/_{2}$ feet to $6^{1}/_{2}$ feet according
to species. (Zone 10)

Azolla caroliniana
AZOLLA, FAIRY MOSS (fs f o)

A deciduous perennial with
divided fronds, ranging from
red and purple to light blue-green.
Reduces algae in the water. Can
spread vigorously. (Zones 5-6)

Azolla filiculoides
AZOLLA (fs ps f o)

A deciduous perennial fern with
green fronds during spring,
deepening to a rich red in summer
and in autumn. Very hardy and
easy to grow. (Zone 7)

Brasenia schreberi
WATERSHIELD (fs f)

A semi-evergreen perennial with bright
green foliage. It has small maroon
flowers in spring and summer,
which may be submerged.
(Zone 4)

ABOVE: Eye-catching horsetails (Equisetum *sp.*) *are excellent accent or feature plants for the water garden, with tall, vertical segmented stems that vary in hue according to the species. They are vigorous growers and will form a solid clump in one or two seasons.*

Butomus umbellatus
FLOWERING RUSH (fs m)

A deciduous perennial with rush-like narrow foliage of a mid-green shade. Pretty umbels of pink to deep rose-red flowers in summer. Grows from 1^1/$_2$ feet to 4^1/$_2$ feet.
(Zone 5)

Cabomba caroliniana
(ps d o)

A deciduous or semi-evergreen perennial that forms dense clumps of bright green foliage. It grows vigorously, and is suitable for use as an oxygenating plant.
(Zone 5)

Calla palustris
WATER ARUM (fs m)

A deciduous or semi-evergreen perennial forming a spreading cover of glossy mid to dark green leaves. Has showy, large white spathes in spring, followed by red or orange fruit. Grows to 10 inches.
(Zone 2)

Caltha leptosepala
(fs m)

Deciduous to semi-evergreen perennial that forms hummocks of deep green foliage, and produces small white flowers in spring. Grows and spreads to 1 foot.
(Zone 3)

Caltha palustris
MARSH MARIGOLD (fs m)

A deciduous or semi-evergreen perennial with rounded dark green leaves. In spring it has cup-like golden yellow flowers in bright clusters. Grows and spreads to 1 foot. (Zone 3)

Canna sp.
CANNA LILY (fs m or e)

An attractive group of vigorous perennials, often with striking foliage as well as flowers. Flowers vary from brilliant red to yellow or salmon pink, while the foliage can be bronze-green or cream and green variegated.

Carex morrowii
(fs m)

A hardy and vigorously growing sedge, useful as a protective bordering plant. It has decorative spikes of brownish flowers in summer. Generally grows up to $3^{1}/_{4}$ feet but can reach $6^{1}/_{2}$ feet. Can be invasive. (Zone 6)

Carex perdula
SEDGE GRASS(fs m)

An evergreen perennial that forms dense tufts of pale yellowish green foliage. During spring tiny bright spikelets appear. Grows up to 2–5 feet. and can be very vigorous. (Zones 6-8)

Ceratopteris thalictroides
WATER FERN (fs d or f)

A semi-evergreen perennial water fern with willowy soft green fronds of heart-shaped foliage, usually carried on the water's surface. (Zone 10)

Colocasia esculenta
TARO (ps m)

A deciduous to semi-evergreen perennial with striking mid or dark green veined foliage. Also a variety with purple-spotted leaves. Grows to $3^{1}/_{2}$ feet and spreads to 2 feet. (Zone 9)

Cotula coronopifolia
BRASS-BUTTONS (fs m)

A deciduous to evergreen short-lived plant with thick fleshy stems and small mid-green leaves. Has pretty button-shaped yellow flower heads for many months of the year. Grows and spreads to 1 foot. (Zone 7)

Crassula
SWAMP CRASSULA (fs ps m)

A low-growing plant that forms a dense mat of attractive foliage. Has small white flowers in summer, and a vigorous spreading growth habit in water up to a depth of about 1 foot. (Zones 9-10)

Cyperus alternifolius
UMBRELLA PLANT, UMBRELLA PALM (fs m or e)

An evergreen perennial sedge with tufts of dark green foliage and clustered spikes of tiny white flowers in summer. Grows to $3^{1}/_{4}$ feet and spreads to 1 foot. (Zone 10)

Cyperus papyrus
PAPYRUS (fs m)

An evergreen perennial sedge that forms a spreading clump of tough leafless stems. Brown spikelets appear in summer. Grows from 10 feet to 16 feet. (Zone 9)

Dryopteris thelypteris
MARSH FERN (ps b or e)

A small-growing semi-evergreen fern that prefers acid soil and moist, shady conditions. A pretty accent plant in the right spot.

Eichhornia crassipes
WATER HYACINTH (fs d)

A vigorous plant with mid-green foliage and spectacular rosy-lilac, pink or mauve flowers. Considered a pest in large ponds. Use with caution. (Zone 8)

ABOVE: One of the most appealing foliage plants is the hosta (Hosta sp.), which grows into a large clump that thrives in rich moist soil. Foliage varies considerably in size and hue according to the variety, and there are some excellent variegated forms with cream and bright green leaves.

Eleocharis dulcis
CHINESE WATER CHESTNUT
(fs m)

A perennial rush with a vigorous spreading growth habit. It produces edible tubers, and has narrow mid-green leaves. (Zone 7)

Equisetum hyemale
HORSETAIL RUSH (fs ps m)

A striking plant with rigid, upright segmented stems in a delicate silvery blue, topped with decorative cones. It is a vigorous growing species, reaching 2 feet in height. (Zone 3)

Euphorbia sp.
(ps e)

A group of useful perennials that enjoy the rich moist soil conditions that are found near ponds or streams. Good drainage is essential. A wide range of foliage and flowers according to the species.

Filipendula ulmaria
COMMON MEADOWSWEET,
QUEEN-OF-THE-MEADOW
(fs ps e)

A perennial forming clumps of large divided leaves that are often fern-like in appearance. During summer it bears frothy panicles of flowers that are white or pale pink. Some varieties grow to a height of 6½ feet. (Zones 2-3)

Filipendula vulgaris
DROPWORT (fs ps e)

An upright perennial with fern-like foliage and fleshy swollen roots. The flowers are white, flushed with pink, and appear in summer. Grows to a height of 6½ feet. (Zone 3)

Geranium sp.
CRANESBILL (fs or ps e)

A charming group of perennials for planting in well-drained beds adjacent to the pond. There are many varieties, in a wide range of foliage sizes and flower hues; they look attractive when mass planted or mingled with other perennials.

Geum rivale
WATER AVENS (fs e)

A perennial that forms clumps of dark green leaves with a furry texture. In spring and summer it has drooping bell-shaped flowers of a creamy pink, flushed with orange. Grows to 1 foot. (Zone 3)

Gunnera manicata
CHILEAN RHUBARB (fs e)

A perennial with enormous deep green leaves that have toothed edges. In early summer it produces conical light green flower heads, followed by orange-brown seed pods. Grows to 6½ feet and spreads to 7 feet. (Zone 7)

Hemerocallis sp.
DAY LILY (fs ps e)

A perennial, generally of vigorous growth, that form clumps of strap-shaped, mid-green leaves. Flowers spring or summer and vary from white to lemon-yellow to rose-red. Grows from 1½ feet to 3¼ feet tall, and spreads to 3¼ feet. (Zones 2-9)

Hibiscus moschuetos
SWAMP HIBISCUS (fs m)

A handsome shrub growing to 4 feet with mid-green foliage and showy flowers that are in the red, pink, and white range of hues.

Hosta sp.
PLANTAIN LILY (ps b or e)

A group of perennials featuring large clumps of beautiful foliage. They have slender spikes of tiny mauve to violet flowers during summer, and grow from 2 feet to 3¼ feet. (Zone 3)

Houttuynia cordata
CHAMELEON (ps m)

A deciduous perennial that forms a mass of aromatic leathery foliage. During spring, small spikes of flowers are produced. These are surrounded by white oval bracts. Grows to 2 feet. (Zones 3-8)

Hydrocharis
(fs f)

A deciduous perennial with small, kidney-shaped, olive-green leaves forming dense rosettes. Produces tiny white flowers in summer. Can form a mass 3¼ feet in diameter.

Hydrocleys nymphoides
WATER POPPY (fs d)

A deciduous to semi-evergreen perennial with rounded mid-green leaves carried on or above the water's surface. During summer, poppy-like yellow flowers appear above the foliage. Spreads to 2 feet. (Zone 10)

Iris ensata
SWORD-LEAVED IRIS (fs m or b)

A group of very beautiful beardless irises that grow to 3 feet in height, with branched stems and purple or purple-red flowers from late spring to early summer.

Iris laevigata
BLUE FLAG IRIS, RABBIT EAR IRIS (fs ps m or e)

A beardless rhizomatous perennial in a number of different forms. Generally has mid-green foliage with branching stems and blue, white, or red flowers. Grows from 2 feet to 3¼ feet. (Zone 4)

Iris pseudacorus
YELLOW IRIS (fs m or b)

A rhizomatous perennial with ridged silvery green leaves in upright clumps. Branching stems produce golden yellow flowers in early spring. Grows to $6^1/2$ feet. (Zone 5)

Juncus effusus
SOFTRUSH (fs b or e)

An upright plant with tufts of fine delicate foliage. In spring, pale green flower heads are produced. Grows vigorously, and will thrive in boggy areas if the soil dries out during summer. (Zone 3)

Lemna minor
DUCKWEED (fs f)

A semi-evergreen perennial that forms a floating carpet of tiny mid-green foliage. Often grown in with other floating plants. Spreads to $3^1/4$ feet on the water's surface. (Zone 4)

Liatris spicata
BUTTON SNAKE-ROOT, SPIKE GAYFEATHER (fs e)

A perennial that forms clumps of lacy, mid to dark green foliage. The rosy pink flower heads are carried on thick erect stems in late summer. Grows to 2 feet. (Zone 3)

Ligularia dentata
BIG LEAF GOLDEN-RAY (fs ps e)

A compact clump-forming perennial with leathery, dark green-brown foliage. During summer it produces loose heads of orange-yellow flowers. Grows to $3^3/4$ feet. (Zone 5)

Lobellia cardinalis
CARDINAL FLOWER (fs ps e)

A perennial that forms clumps of green or rust-bronze foliage. From mid to late summer it has brilliant scarlet flowers. Grows to a height of $3^1/4$ feet. (Zone 2)

Lysichiton camtschatcensis
WHITE SKUNK CABBAGE (fs m or b)

A deciduous perennial with spikes of tiny white flowers and snow-white spathes in spring. The foliage is an attractive bright green. Grows to $2^1/2$ feet. (Zone 6)

Lysimachia nummularia
CREEPING JENNY, MONEYWORT (fs e)

A low-growing perennial that forms a loose carpet of bright green leaves. During summer it has heads of small, cup-shaped, bright yellow flowers. Spreads to 1 foot. (Zone 3)

Lysimachia vulgaris
YELLOW LOOSESTRIFE (fs ps e)

A perennial suitable for the border of a water garden. Thrives in moist, but well-drained soil and produces plumes of golden yellow flowers during summer. Grows and spreads to 1 foot. (Zone 5)

Lythrum salicaria
PURPLE LOOSESTRIFE (fs e)

A clump-forming perennial with mid-green leaves on slender stems. Some varieties produce spikes of magenta to rose-red blooms during summer. Grows to a height of $3^1/4$ feet. (Zone 3)

Marsilea drummondii
WATER CLOVER (fs m)

An evergreen fern with clover-like fronds, that can be held above the water or floating. They are a delicate silver-green and are furry to touch. Spreads rapidly and grows to 1 foot. (Zone 10)

Mazus pumilio
SWAMP MAZUS (fs e)

A deciduous or evergreen perennial that becomes a spreading carpet of light green leaf rosettes. Through spring and summer it has purple to pink or white flowers on slender stems. Grows to 2 inches. (Zone 7)

Mentha
MINT (fs ps e)

A group of attractive and useful perennials prized for their aromatic culinary foliage. Plant with caution as they can become invasive. Most bear small mauve to purple flowers during summer. Height varies according to species. (Zone 3)

Menyanthes trifoliata
BOGBEAN, MARSH TREFOIL (fs m or b)

A deciduous perennial with large mid-green leaves carried on dark fleshy stems. In spring and summer white fringed flowers appear. Grows to 10 inches and spreads to 1 foot. (Zone 3)

Myosotis scorpioides
WATER FORGET-ME-NOT (fs m)

A semi-evergreen perennial that becomes a spreading mound of tiny mid-green leaves. During summer it produces tiny blue flowers. Very similar to its land-loving relatives. Grows to 1 foot. (Zone 3)

Myriophyllum aquaticum
PARROT'S FEATHER (fs d o)

A deciduous or evergreen perennial with a wide, spreading growth habit. The feathery blue-green foliage may turn red in cool climates if it grows above water. Grows to 9 inches. (Zone 10)

ABOVE: Yellow irises (Iris pseudacorus) *can be grown in a bog garden, or as a marginal planting near the edge of a pool. It has silvery green foliage and stems of brilliant golden yellow flowers in spring.*

ABOVE: Tropical waterlilies (Nymphaea sp.) require warm growing conditions, as their name suggests. Plant in containers in a rich mixture of good garden loam and well-aged cow manure, and submerge to a depth equal to the length of the foliage stems.

Myriophyllum verticillatum WHIRLED WATER MILFOIL (fs d o)

A deciduous to evergreen perennial with slender submerged stems. These are covered with a dense covering of delicate olive green leaves, which sometimes grow above water level. Various sizes. (Zone 3)

Nelumbo lutea AMERICAN LOTUS (fs m)

A deciduous perennial with large, blue-green, upright leaves. In summer it has showy yellow flowers that are delightfully fragrant. One of the most delightful water plants. Very vigorous, grows up to 6½ feet tall. (Zones 4-10)

Nelumbo nucifera SACRED LOTUS (fs m)

A deciduous tropical perennial from Australia, with enormous blue-green floating leaves. Large rose-pink flowers are produced in summer. Grows from 3 feet to 5 feet above the water's surface. (Zones 4-10)

Nuphar luteum YELLOW WATER LILY (ps d)

A deciduous perennial for still ponds or running streams, with leathery mid-green leaves. Grows

very rapidly, and needs a large pond as it spreads to 5 feet. Produces small, bottle-shaped yellow flowers in summer, followed by seed heads.
(Zone 4)

Nymphaea sp.
WATERLILY (fs d)

The most popular and widely grown water plants, these lilies are either deciduous or evergreen perennials with large, rounded floating leaves and brightly hued flowers. Range in size from miniature varieties spreading only 6 inches to very vigorous cultivars growing up to 10 feet or 13 feet in diameter. Blooms are often fragrant and are produced in a wide range of hues from the classic snowy white to a rich garnet-red. Hardy and tropical varieties, suitable for a wide range of climates.
(Zones 3-10)

Nymphoides indica
WATER SNOWFLAKE
(fs m or d)

A semi-evergreen perennial with large, floating orb-like leaves. Above these, white flowers are produced during summer with delicate fringed edges. Grows to 3 feet, in tropical or sub-tropical conditions only.
(Zone 9)

Nymphoides peltata
WATER FRINGE, FLOATING
HEART (fs m or d)

A deciduous or semi-evergreen perennial with mid-green floating foliage. During summer small, fringed yellow flowers are produced above the rounded leaves. Spreads to 2 feet, and must have warm growing conditions.
(Zone 5)

Orontium aquaticum
GOLDEN CLUB (fs d or f)

Deciduous to semi-evergreen perennial with glossy, floating or slightly emergent foliage. Golden flowers are borne above the surface in spring. Spreads to 2 feet.
(Zone 7)

Osmunda regalis
ROYAL FERN (ps m or e)

A beautiful deciduous fern with large fronds of bright green foliage, growing in height to 5 feet. When mature, the fern carries rusty brown flower spikes in summer.

Ottelia alismoides
SWAMP LILY (fs f)

A tropical perennial or annual water plant with elliptical leaves that form a carpet on the

water's surface. The white blooms are maroon in the middle and are produced during spring and summer. Can spread over 3 feet.
(Zone 9)

Pistia stratiotes
WATER LETTUCE (fs f)

A deciduous, perennial floating plant with lettuce-like foliage. Suitable for pools and aquariums, it has a small spread and should not be cultivated below 50°F. Remove fading foliage as necessary.
(Zone 8)

Polygonatum multiflorum
SOLOMON'S SEAL (ps e)

A leafy perennial with arching mid-green leaves and pretty clusters of green-tipped white flowers in late spring. Likes cool moist conditions. Grows to 3 feet.
(Zones 2-3)

Pontederia cordata
PICKEREL WEED, PICKEREL
RUSH (fs m)

A deciduous upright perennial with glossy dark green foliage and dense spikes of tiny blue flowers on fleshy stems in summer. Popular and easy to grow. Grows to 2³/4 feet.
(Zone 3)

ABOVE: The red canna lily is often seen growing at the water's edge, with mid-green foliage and tall stems of dramatic bright red flowers. Cannas cannot be grown in cold climates, but thrive in temperate and warm zones in a sunny position in rich moist soil.

Pratia
(ps e)

A prostrate creeping perennial with small dark green leaves. In spring and early summer a mass of pale to mid-blue flowers are produced. Has a vigorous spreading capacity.
(Zone 7)

Primula beesiana
BEES PRIMROSE (fs ps e)

A perennial with slender toothed leaves. In early summer it has purple to lilac blooms that look pretty at the water's edge. Grows from 1¹/₂ feet to 2 feet.
(Zone 6)

Primula florindae
PRIMULA (fs m or e)

A delightful showy plant that can be grown in marginal areas or in the rich peaty soil on the edge of a stream. The bell-like sulphur yellow flowers appear in summer, and form a handsome clump up to 3 feet in height.

Primula florindae
TIBETAN PRIMROSE (fs ps e)

An erect clump-forming perennial with oval mid-green leaves. Has showy large heads of bell-like sulphur-yellow flowers in summer. Grows from 2 feet to 3 feet.
(Zone 5)

Primula japonica
JAPANESE PRIMROSE
(fs ps e)

An upright perennial with coarse

pale-green leaves. Rich red blooms are produced on thick stems from spring to early summer. Grows up to 2 feet. (Zone 5)

Ranunculus
BUTTERCUP
(fs ps m b or d)

These plants take different forms, some with fine narrow leaves and others with broad glossy foliage. Small yellow flowers are produced in spring and summer. Small fish like to shelter in the foliage. (Zone 5)

Ranunculus lingua
(fs m)

A deciduous perennial with thick stems that emerge above the waterline, and narrow dark green leaves. Clusters of yellow flowers in late spring, grows to 3 feet by 1^1/$_2$ feet. (Zone 4)

Rodgersia pinnata

A clump-forming hardy perennial that likes rich moist soil conditions. Grows to 5 feet in height, with mid-green foliage and dense panicles of bright pink feathery flowers.

Sagittaria sagittifolia
'Florepleno'
COMMON ARROWHEAD (fs m)

A deciduous perennial with mid-green leaves in a distinct arrow-like shape.

The white flowers are rich purple in the middle and bloom in summer. Grows to 1^1/$_2$ feet. (Zone 5)

Sarracenia sp.
PITCHER PLANT
(ps m or b)

A group of fascinating insectivorous perennials which can be grown as small feature plants on the edge of a shaded pond. Cannot withstand frost, and must have slightly acid soil to survive. Wide range of varieties available.

Saururus cernuus
LIZARD'S TAIL (fs m b)

A deciduous perennial that forms dense clumps of mid-green leaves. In summer it produces racemes of tiny creamy flowers, borne above the foliage. Grows from 1 foot to 2^3/$_4$ feet. (Zone 5)

Sparganium erectum
BRANCHED BUR REED (ps m)

A deciduous or semi-evergreen perennial admired for its narrow mid-green leaves. In summer it has small green-brown burs in spikes among the foliage. Grows to 3^1/$_4$ feet. (Zone 6)

Thalia dealbata
WATER CANNA (fs m)

A deciduous perennial with long-

stalked foliage and spikes of purple blooms in summer, if grown in a warm position. Grows to 3^1/$_4$ feet. (Zone 7)

Thalictrum dipterocarpum
MEADOW RUE (fs ps e)

A perennial that forms hummocks of divided mid-green leaves above which panicles of drooping lilac blooms appear from mid to late summer. It grows to 3^1/$_2$ feet. (Zone 4)

Thalictrum flavum
COMMON MEADOW RUE
(fs ps e)

A perennial that creates an excellent pool border of thick divided foliage. The blooms lack petals, but have fluffy clusters of stamens with mauve sepals in spring. Grows to 3^1/$_4$ feet. (Zone 6)

Triglochin
ARROW GRASS (fs d or b)

A rhizomatous evergreen perennial with floating or erect foliage. Dense spikes of small green flowers are borne above the water in spring and summer. (Zones 5-8)

Typha latifolia
CATTAIL (fs m)

A deciduous perennial that grows into large clumps of mid-green foliage. It has spikes of beige flowers in late summer, followed by cylindrical rich brown seed heads. Grows to 6½ feet and spreads to 2 feet. (Zone 3)

Utricularia vulgaris
BLADDERWORT (fs m d)

A deciduous or evergreen perennial that becomes a delicate network of branches beneath the water. In summer, masses of brilliant yellow flowers are borne above the waterline. Grows to a size of 1¾ feet. (Zone 7)

Vallisneria spiralis
EELGRASS, TAPE GRASS (fs ps d)

An evergreen perennial that grows quickly, forming a mass of willowy mid-green leaves. Small green flowers all year round. (Zone 8)

Zantedeschia aethiopica
LILY OF THE NILE (fs m or e)

A handsome plant that forms a dense clump of mid-green foliage and produces tall stems of pure white flowers with a yellow spadix. Very easy to grow in a wide range of soils and conditions.

ABOVE: St. Louis Gold is a very reliable, easy-to-grow waterlily with deep golden yellow flowers that bloom in abundance over many weeks in summer. It can be adapted to quite small pools, and will not become too vigorous or invasive.

Index

Photography credits

Front cover: Charles Mann (Tintinhull House Garden, Somerset); Back cover: Mary Moody; Endpapers: Lynn Karlin;
Title page: Charles Mann (Chaunard Garden); Page 4: Charles Mann; Page 5: Charles Mann; Page 6: Jerry Harpur (Designer Mirabel Osler);
Page 8: Clive Nichols (Blenheim Palace, Oxfordshire); Pages 10–11: Clive Nichols (Jardins de la fondation ephrussi de Rothschild, France);
Page 12: Charles Mann (Hestercombe, England); Page 13: Charles Mann; Page 14: Mary Moody;
Pages 16–17: Charles Mann (Tintinhull House Garden, Somerset); Page 18: Jerry Harpur (Designer Christopher Masson);
Page 22: Charles Mann (Briskey); Page 24: Clive Nichols (Tintinhull House Garden, Somerset); Page 25: Charles Mann (Tintinhull House Garden, Somerset); Page 28: Jerry Harpur (Julian Elliott, Capetown S.A.); Page 32: Harry Smith Collection (Chelsea); Page 34: Peter Baistow;
Page 35: Gil Hanley; Page 38: Clive Nichols (Preen Manor Garden, Shropshire); Page 42: Charles Mann; Page 46: Charles Mann (Designer Allan Mandell); Page 50: Mary Moody; Page 52: Jerry Harpur (Japanese garden, Long Island); Page 53: Australian Design Series Magazines (ACP Publishing Pty Ltd)/Warwick Kent; Page 56: Charles Mann (Clapton Court); Page 58: Peter Baistow (Sutton Place); Page 59: Peter Baistow;
Pages 62–63: Clive Nichols (Babbacombe Model Village, Devon); Page 64: Clive Nichols (Lower Severalls, Somerset); Page 66: Charles Mann;
Page 69: Gil Hanly; Page 70: Charles Mann; Page 71: Charles Mann; Pages 72–73: Clive Nichols (The Crossing House, Shepreth, Hertfordshire);
Page 74: S. & O. Mathews; Page 76: Charles Mann (E. Scott); Page 78: Charles Mann (Designer Allan Mandell, Santa Fe); Page 79: S. & O. Mathews;
Page 80: Mary Moody; Page 81: Charles Mann (Hadspen House); Page 82: Peter Baistow; Page 83: Clive Nichols (La Mortola Garden, Italy);
Pages 84–85: Clive Nichols (Bodnant Garden, Wales); Page 86: Clive Nichols (Brook Cottage, Oxfordshire);
Page 88: Clive Nichols (Exbury Gardens, Hampshire); Page 89: Clive Nichols (Brook Cottage, Oxfordshire);
Page 91: Clive Nichols (Brook Cottage, Oxfordshire); Page 92: Mary Moody; Page 93: Charles Mann; Pages 94–95: Clive Nichols (Brook Cottage, Oxfordshire); Page 96: Clive Nichols (Woodland Garden, Exbury, Hampshire); Page 98: Charles Mann; Page 99: Mary Moody;
Page 100: Clive Nichols (Wolfson College Gardens, Oxford); Page 101: Clive Nichols (Brook Cottage, Oxfordshire); Page 102: Charles Mann;
Page 103: Clive Nichols (Exbury Gardens, Hampshire); Pages 104–105: S. & O. Mathews; Page 106: Charles Mann;
Page 109: The Image Bank/Derek Berwin; Pages 110–111: Charles Mann; Page 112: Charles Mann; Page 114: Charles Mann;
Page 116: Charles Mann; Page 119: Charles Mann; Page 120: Charles Mann; Page 122: Charles Mann; Page 124: Mary Moody

---

ZONE RATINGS

The zone rating refers to the minimum temperature a plant will tolerate.

Zone 1	-50°F	Zone 6	0°F
Zone 2	-40°F	Zone 7	10°F
Zone 3	-30°F	Zone 8	20°F
Zone 4	-20°F	Zone 9	30°F
Zone 5	-10°F	Zone 10	40°F
	Zone 11	above 40°F	

Meredith ® Books
President, Book Group: Joseph J. Ward
Vice President and Editorial Director: Elizabeth P. Rice
Executive Editor: Nancy N. Green
Art Director: Ernest Shelton

Published by Lansdowne Publishing Pty Limited,
70 George Street, Sydney, NSW, 2000, Australia.

Project Editor: Deborah Nixon
Designer: Kathie Baxter-Smith
Illustrator: Valerie Price

Meredith Corporation Corporate Officers:
Chairman of the Executive Committee: E.T. Meredith III
Chairman of the Board, President
and Chief Executive Officer: Jack D. Rehm
Group Presidents:
Joseph J. Ward, Books
William T. Kerr, Magazines
Philip A. Jones, Broadcasting
Allen L. Sabbag, Real Estate
Vice Presidents:
Leo R. Armatis, Corporate Relations
Thomas G. Fisher, General Counsel and Secretary
Larry D. Hartsook, Finance
Michael A. Sell, Treasurer
Kathleen J. Zehr, Controller and Assistant Secretary

First Published 1993
by Lansdowne Publishing Pty Limited
First printed in the U.S.A. in 1994
© Copyright Lansdowne Publishing Pty Limited 1993
© Copyright design Lansdowne Publishing Pty Limited 1993

Library of Congress Catalog Card Number: 93-86610
ISBN: 0-696-00098-9

Designed on Quark Express in 11.3 pt Garamond 3
Printed in Singapore by Kyodo Printing Co. (S'pore) Pty Ltd.

Front cover: This well-established formal water garden imparts a feeling of tranquil timelessness.

Back cover: Waterlilies (Nymphaea sp.)

Endpapers: Spring blossom trees reflected in the lake, edged by stone and grassy banks.

Title page: The warm yellows and greens of lady's mantle (Alchemilla mollis) beside a tranquil pond set in a cottage garden landscape.

Page 4: Thriving ground-cover plants between rocks surrounding an informal concrete-lined pond.

Contents page: Waterlilies (Nymphaea sp.) are the most popular flowering water plant, requiring an open, sunny position.